VIGNETTES

JOSIP NOVAKOVICH

Montreal Publishing Company

ISBN: 978-1-7386548-3-3

Vignettes—1st edition.
Editor: Christian Fennell
Copyeditor: Nathalie Guilbeault

For privacy reasons, some names, locations, and dates may have been changed.

Front cover: Nelligan Design
Montreal Publishing Company
montrealpublishing.com

JOSIP NOVAKOVICH

Novakovich emigrated from Croatia at the age of 20. His work has been anthologized in Best American Poetry, the Pushcart Prize and O. Henry Prize Stories. He has received the Whiting Writer's Award, a Guggenheim fellowship, the Ingram Merrill Award and an American Book Award. In 2013 Josip was a Man Booker International Award finalist. He teaches creative writing at Concordia University in Montreal.

Other Books by Josip Novakovich

Rubble of Rubles
Honey in the Carcase: Stories
Heritage of Smoke
Shopping for a Better Country
Three Deaths
April Fool's Day: A Novel
Infidelities: Stories of War and Lust
Fiction Writer's Workshop
Plum Brandy
Fiction Writing Step by Step
Salvation and Other Disasters
Ex-YU
Tumbleweed
Apricots from Chernobyl

Acclaim for Josip Novakovich's
Rubble of Rubles

"Throughout the madcap plotting, a pervasive sense of menace never dissipates. An international comedy of errors that ventures to knowingly bleak places."

– *Kirkus Starred Review*

. . . in vertiginous scenes that evoke Kafka, Dostoyevsky, and Alice in Wonderland, the police and prison officials subject David to extortion, drugging, and interrogation, and even Putin himself gets a cartoonish and nightmarish cameo. Not only is this sickeningly surreal, it's a hell of a ride.

– *Publisher's Weekly, Starred Review*

"Hints of allegory are never far from the surface in Novakovich's frightening and darkly hilarious new novel *Rubble of Rubles*. Full of colour, savage humour, and absurdity, it is a worthy addition to the best books about Russia. There are surreal touches that bring to mind Bulgakov's *The Master and Margarita*, as well as the kind of modern grit you might find in Martin Cruz Smith's series of Russian detective novels. . . .A highly entertaining read full of substance, madness, and whip-smart observations."

– *Montreal Review of Books*

"Josip Novakovich's narrative style—powerfully direct, crisply precise, bluntly confident without arrogance—is instantly recognizable and entirely sui generis. No single sentence goes to waste in his texts, no word a throwaway one. His prose resonates with distant rhythms of faraway histories. He is one of the preeminent storytellers of our time—and one of the very best we have. In this remarkable, highly immersive novel, set in the early-aughts Russia poised on the cusp of becoming the moral catastrophe of a state it is today, his satire is cutting and unswerving, his gaze steadfast and uncommonly, uncannily observant."

– Mikhail Iossel, author of Every Hunter Wants to Know

"In a thrilling mix of an adventure novel and satire, Josip Novakovich provides us with a fresh glimpse into that horrifying and mysterious Russian soul. So relevant that it's scary!"

– Lara Vapnyar, author of Divide Me By Zero

"Josip Novakovich's latest novel is a tour de force that exposes the complete corruption of the Russian police and legal system under Putin. David Dvornik is an insomniac, former investment banker, Russophile, amateur historian, and ex graduate student from Yale, who uses sarcasm and farce to describe the absurdity of his daily life in Saint Petersburg. Novakovich turns the idea of Crime and Punishment on its head. Rather than the inevitable capture of the guilty, we see the inevitable punishment of the innocent."

– Josh Barkan, author of Mexico: Stories

"Crime and the lack of punishment - Josip Novakovich conjures up a picture of Saint Petersburg that would terrify Dostoevsky."

– Tibor Fischer, author of Under the Frog

"*Rubble of Rubles* shows Josip Novakovich at his best. I know of no other writer who knows how to ridicule the ridiculous and find meaning in the seemingly meaningless. This is a comic novel with serious content, rich in dark humor and startling cultural insights."

– Jim Heynan, author of One-Room Schoolhouse

"This novel took hold of me from the beginning and never let go. Kafkaesque for the first two-thirds, and then something else. I am not sure what: maybe a bit of the Wizard of Oz, and a bit Hitchcock, with a happy ending. I shall never think of Russia the same way, or of Georgian wine. A timely book filled with humor and twists and turns."

– Robert Appelbaum, author of Terrorism Before the Letter: Mythography and Political Violence in England, Scotland, and France 1559-1642

CONTENTS

INTRODUCTION

So, I have been writing WINE anecdotes and wondering how to genre them, when it occurred to me that vine preceded genre and gave birth to vignette, a beautiful term which has since been demolished by flash fiction, prose poem, lyrical essay, short-shorts, sudden fiction, and other bull. Nevertheless, being primitive, kind of a fundamentalist Baptist, I tend to the basics here, and so, a bit of wine, in a small glass, a bit of truth, in a few lines, works for me.

If it's not as boring as a sermon—but wait a minute, sermons in my church went on for hours as the spirit moved these speakers, and a vine vignette won't torment that long, it lasts as long as a good glass of wine, or rather, much less, a minute or two, as long as a gulp and its shades of red. This is what I found on vignette online—pardon me, I have no time to walk to the New York Public Library or the British something or other to be more thorough, and now Covid-21 gives me an excuse: Vignette: 1751, "decorative design," originally a design in the form of vine tendrils around the borders of a book page, especially a picture page, from French vignette, from Old French diminutive of vigne "vineyard" (see vine). Sense transferred from the border to the picture itself, then (1853) to a type of small photographic portrait with blurred edges very popular mid-19c. Meaning "literary sketch" is first recorded 1880, probably from the photographic sense. Etc.

Wine in my childhood was a mysterious liquid. Daruvar, my hometown, was surrounded by vineyards; wine was everywhere, almost as much as beer. But we were the center of the Czech minorities in Yugoslavia and had one of the oldest breweries in the country, *Staročeška pivovara*. For a while the signs were not only in two scripts, Cyrillic and Latin, to reconcile Serbs and Croats, but also in Czech, to appease the Czechs and to demonstrate that we were not a god-forsaken hick town, but rather a cosmopolitan haven, and so Gornji Daruvar, or Upper Daruvar, was spelled as Horni Daruvar, Horni being gornji, or upper. The United Nations peacekeepers drew a lot of merriment from the unintended pun. Maybe if the wine had been better there would have been no war. I could smell the wine spilled on floorboards wafting from various taverns, and even worse, the smells of Daruvarski Riesling rising through the floors of my elementary school in an old castle on a hill, two hundred meters from a house in which I was born, the old-fashioned way—midwife delivery. There were barrels of whites and some reds; through the cracks of the barrels my peers and I learned the basics of math, grammar, history, and literature, somewhat dizzy and fumigated in wine vapors that seeped upward through the oiled oak floors. At home, we had a little vineyard, from which we ate Noah's grapes, and my mother made grape juice. My father apparently never drank and satisfied his sugar cravings by keeping bees. He sometimes invited me to linger with him at the entrance of a tavern to look at staggering drunks and to smell the foul fumes, and said, Son, don't ever drink booze.

When I was twelve I read *Death Ship* and the *Treasures of Sierra Madre* by B. Traven. Rum and wine drinking seemed to be what pirates and sailors did. For a whole week I was a pirate and a convict, living in Bruno Traven's imagination, but it was not substantial enough. I wanted to taste the wine. Jesus drinking wine and turning water into wine was not enough of an intrigue for me to taste the wine for the first time, but fiction was. In Zadar, where

I attended a summer camp—nearly all the Yugoslav kids at the time could spend at government expense a month in camps at the coast, swimming, eating sardines, and coming up with nasty things to do. In the evening, with a friend of mine, Boro, we passed by a tavern, with a barrel of wine sporting a wet spigot. The sign said, Glass of Wine 10 Dinars. That's not all that much, I said to Boro, less than an ice-cream. I'm going to taste it, I need to know what the sailors know. You go ahead, Boro said. My father is a drunk and I've seen more than enough of wine. I hate the shit. I went in, and asked for a glass of wine. The bartender said, Son, how old are you? Twelve, I said. Fine, that's old enough, he said. Smart child, you can tell right away, said one of the patrons. I drank one glass as though it were grape juice. I didn't know you were supposed to sip it; I gulped it down. It was surprisingly sour and not pleasing at all. The bartender said, The first glass may taste like that, but the second will be much better. So I had the second one. I stepped outside into the dusk on the cobbles, and the street tiles were somehow more slippery than before. I ran into Boro, and other friends of mine, and I surprised them by speaking in all the Yugoslav dialects I could recall. First Dalmatian, then northern Serbian, then hillbilly Slavonian style, then Zagorje … I could do all these accents and dialects—a skill I lost when I began to speak English, and where I can do only one accent, mine. I don't remember how the evening ended; I woke up sick the following morning and had no interest in wine for the next twelve years. I also didn't read any more Bruno Traven. Still, wine may have a lot to do with my interest in literature, or it may be the other way around—I am not sure which came first, those vapors, or the stories involving wine?

INSTEAD OF TEATIME, NOSTALGIA FOR RED WINE

That's where my father and I differ, although people tell me we look alike. Namely, he was an herbalist who drank one hundred varieties of tea, which still didn't spare him from a massive heart attack. I wonder whether drinking one hundred varieties of wine would have worked better? And even though cardiology has advanced since those days, when I had the honor of traveling to Croatia and Bosnia with photographer Jon Hughes from Cincinnati, he warned me—I will come, but I know the region is famous for unrestrained drinking, and I want none of that—I've had heart failure, and I must carefully balance my chemistry with Lipitor and amlodipine, cholesterol and blood pressure meds. I will not drink in your fucking country. Jon, why would I care? Drink tea if you like, there's lots of it. I don't plan to drink anything either, you know.

I already had a couple of glasses of red wine on our flight to relieve my anxiety. I couldn't do that, Jon said. He took melatonin and slept through the entire flight. We rented a car in Frankfurt, and he drove at first as I hadn't slept.

One of our first stops was Vodnjan, to visit my friend Boris. Boris said, Dudes, you look like the road sucked the life out of you. I'll get you some wine from our neighbor.

He went to the shop next door and brought four liters of red wine and declared that the whole deal was only four bucks.

Why so much wine? asked Jon. I ain't gonna drink none of it.

Oh shush, I said. You never know. I will. I tasted it. It was simple, airy, like some kind of Bourgogne or Beaujolais. One gulp was lonely and it begged for another, and I downed an entire refreshing glass, and said to Jon, All right, my friend, just have a sip. I swear, the wine is thin, won't affect your heart at all.

You know, you sluts, he said, you have aroused my curiosity, and he tasted the wine from a regular water glass, and said, Oh well, I've blown my wine cherry. I haven't had a sip in a year and here I go. My doctor would not be happy.

Of course, he'd be happy, I said. Either you earn another bypass or you get cured. Either he makes a ton of money off of you, or he can boast that he's a good doctor. And what do you think he would do? WWJD? Is that it, What would Jesus do? He would drink some and talk to his dad. Well, I envy him there, I can't talk to mine, but that's beside the point? Refill?

Oh yeah, said Jon, and smiled and his eyes vanished and his mustache spread its wings like a vulture in Texas. I have no idea why I said Texas, but who cares.

Anyway, I went back to the store before it would close, and the young man put more wine into one and a half-litre Coca-Cola bottles. Boris's neighbor, sitting on the steps on the hot night in a wife-beater shirt, looked at me, and said, Why red wine? White is better.

That's a matter of taste, I said.

Is there something wrong with your blood? My wife is anemic, although she now and then flares up and throws things at me, and she doesn't look anemic to me, but the doctor says she is, and prescribes red wine. If something's wrong with your blood, you drink red wine. But just to relax and cool off, of course, you drink white.

So what's your favorite? I asked.

I have none. I hate all alcohol and haven't had a sip of that shit in my entire life. I've seen what it does to people.

OK, so why talk to me about it? I wanted to say in unprintable text, but he looked so good and meek and soulful, sitting on the second stone stair in his red shorts.

Jon must have had two liters or three traditional bottles of red wine. He said, you know, I am sorry and I am not. I feel good.

In the morning, he said again, I feel good. Can we drink more of that?

Then we drove to Sarajevo. I stressed Jon out by driving on Jadranska magistrala, before the new highways, very competitively, and he said, You pass another car like that in a curve and I am out of here. Oh no, you aren't. We have that tranquilizing wine, I said.

1997, Mostar. We drove there and … it was a little stressful. I won't go into details.

We came to Sarajevo and our concept of a present was ten liters of the domestic wine from Istria, and my nephew, a Baptist minister, said, You know, usually I would say no as we are pretty strict with alcohol here, but I am so nostalgic for Croatia, that I accept your gift with gratitude.

Jon and I drank our present to him and his church, at least half of it, a little sheepishly, but Jon said, Man, I miss this wine.

No, you don't. You are drinking it!

Jon and I drove from Sarajevo to Orasje to cross into Croatia, and we were going to pass through Republika Srpska. I didn't know there wasn't a checkpoint between the two parts of Bosnia. I had a book listing 3,000 slain Croatian civilians by Serbian forces in Croatia. I thought if the Serbian police searched us, they might not appreciate such a book, and I tossed it in the curve into the bushes. Republika Srpska was quiet; several orthodox churches were being built. An old man walked two pigs on the side of the road, grazing in grassy ditches. I feel sorry for the pigs, I said. Probably some holiday is coming up and he's gonna bake them.

In Orasje, we waited for a ferry to cross the river Sava, in diesel clouds of tractor trailers.

Jon said, The beauty is that diesel is not harmful.

I don't believe that. I am getting a headache.

That's just wine withdrawal, Jon said. By the way, I am done with wine. It was good while it lasted, and I would drink more of that fine young red wine, but anyhow, I am done.

I am done, too, I said. The hell with drinking.

On the highway of Brotherhood and Unity in Croatia, I drove a steady 130 km/hour, passing by a column of trucks, which went about eighty. It was already night-time, the sky starry and indigo. A car behind me flashed at me to move over, but I wasn't going to move over and then brake in a small space between two trucks, so I kept going, accelerating to 140. That was not good enough for the BMW, which tailgated and flashed.

That's really uncomfortable, Jon said. He's maybe only a meter behind us.

I pulled to the right lane when I passed the first truck, and I slowed down to 130. The BMW slowed to 130 and drove in parallel. I slowed down to 100, so did the driver. I looked over, and saw a gun, probably an Uzi, pointing at me. The driver was leaning his arm on the chest of a reclining blonde woman. I accelerated, so did he. I was back at 140, so was he. There was no traffic on the road anymore in either direction. Jon said, What the fuck? We are both in the line—he could kill us just like that?

Yeah, who would know. After we are shot he could drive away at 200 km/hour, and nobody would know who dissed us.

Driving can't be that serious, Jon said.

I looked over again, and I couldn't make out the features of the man, other than a bit of the whites of the eyes. But the gun pipe and its black hole were all too clearly visible. There were lamp-posts on the side of the road shedding some light, every 100 meters or so.

He is enjoying this, Jon said. I am not! You think he'll shoot?

I have no idea. The world is full of idiots. This is Texas style road rage.

And we drove like that for a while, accelerating and decelerating, and then he suddenly accelerated to probably more than 220 km/hour and pretty soon was gone.

God, this nearly gave me a heart attack, Jon said. I hope the fucker crashes in the next curve.

I stayed calm through the whole thing because it was all too absurd, and I was not in control. But now I was a bit jittery, and I drove at 110 km/hour the rest of the way.

We came to my mother's place in Daruvar late at night. The bell didn't work, so I threw little stones and my mother opened the window and let us in.

After the usual hugs, she offered us walnut strudels and tea.

Jon asked me to translate to her. Can you ask her whether she has any wine? I am still shaking from our being targeted.

You have any wine, Old Woman?

Yes, local Daruvarski Riesling. But you know, you shouldn't be drinking.

Will white wine do? I asked Jon.

Yes!

I had a glass and Jon had the rest of the bottle. It was quite refreshing, pretty dry, yet fruity, with a bit of apple and persimmon aroma. Jon gulped and then smiled so that his eyes vanished for a while in the folds of his cheeks, and his mustache spread like wings of a bird over Texas.

TWA WINE

While teaching a writing workshop at the Fine Arts Work Center, I invited a friend of mine to join me as I had a whole cottage with three rooms to myself, and to be my guest in the workshop of nonfiction. Captain Mark, now an American Airlines pilot, said he would come at ten in the evening on the first Thursday night, July 18. And so I canceled my other social engagements, such as tea with Howard Norman, and waited in the cottage that very humid and sultry evening. Nothing worked to cool me off, and so I sat in my underwear, waiting for Mark. He didn't show up and it was midnight, and then at one I fell asleep. He rang the bell at two and before him entered a bottle of red wine. Great to see you buddy, take this little token!

Great, let's drink it! Without looking at the label, I uncorked the wine and poured some of it into one coffee cup for him and one for me. Not bad, I said. I tossed it in my mouth and could tell it was a bit dry, on the sour side, but altogether not bad, although not sensational either. What kind of wine is it?

Château Margaux 1996 premier grand cru. The French knew what they were doing. It's so good to see you!

He took his shirt off and put his strapped handgun into his briefcase. I wiggled in my clammy tee shirt and had another gulp. Pretty soon I was close to the end of the bottle, and the wine tasted better and better, and I said, This seems to be better than I thought. I am now awake! Better than coffee. Better than coffee, he chimed. And the last drag of it was suddenly fabulous.

It intrigued me that a flat wine could become so good during the course of an evening or early morning but then such is the power of waking up and drinking. In the morning, for the hell of it, as probably many other petty people do these days after parties, I googled the wine he gave me, and was a little disconcerted to see that the going rate for it now was in the range of $800-$1,000. What the hell, I pissed his fine wine for no reason, just like that! I also read that the wine should be decanted for at least an hour to balance out after long entrapment in the bottle.

Mark, what's up with this wine? Thank you very much, you should have warned me that it was so special!

I thought it would speak for itself, and I wanted to surprise you.

Thanks to Mr. Google, I am surprised. You could have … so how come such good wine?

It's the anniversary of my fiancée's death. She died in the crash of TWA 800, bound for Paris, and I bought a case of the wine. So each anniversary, I drink one bottle.

My God, yes, you told me the story. You were supposed to fly with her and you'd be dead but for some reason you didn't fly with her.

Great to see you, amigo, Mark said.

IN THE YEAR 2525

A dilemma: must an anecdote involving wine be a story or it's OK for it to be a moment? I'll recreate a moment. I ain't brave enough for a story at the moment, cowed by memory. What can I say? Maybe this:

I abhor weddings. The concept is off. You get drunk, loose, and then what? Everybody is a relative, so you can't react to the urges, if there are any. So there are no urges, and I sit resentful that people want me to drink and dance. No, I shall do neither. I remember a wedding my cousin, eight years my elder, had in Daruvar. He was the first rock musician in town, a lead guitarist, with flared jeans, an irrepressible smile, long curly black hair, and cowboy boots with exceedingly high heels as he was short. I don't remember the bride. I remember only vaguely that she was good looking. But she was family already, so better not look. Ike and Tina Turner sang on vinyl. And then some dudes from Nebraska, "In the year 2525, if man is still alive, if a woman can survive..." I was fourteen. A lot had already happened. Jimi Hendrix had died and shortly afterward another Jim, Morrison. My father had died before all of them. My world was shattered and strangely it opened up with blinding sunlight. Cousin Mrvica (Crumb) was getting married. Anyhow, I observed dancing, and thought, Why are Jimi and Jim and Father dead? They could play more provocative music. But maybe they couldn't. If the year 2525 was apocalyptic. "In the year 7510... I guess it's time for Judgment Day." The song sent a shiver of doom down my skin and to my narrow Italian shoes. My balding and flushed uncle was playing the guitar and sweat sparked off him. His blind wife smiled revealing big white teeth and one gold one and swayed in the rhythm. My female cousin, with amazingly thick black hair, married to a Hungarian welter-weight boxing finalist from Argentina, who was no longer welter-weight, danced, drank and laughed … I had no idea that only Mrvica, I, and Sonyi, the boxer, would be alive a few decades later. My cousin Nina died in excruciating pain from lupus a few years after the wedding. Mrvica lives alone. Most of the party was felled by horrifying luck. And somehow I had the premonition. I sat there, gloomy as a night forest in November. Very few of my other cousins were there, although we were a very cousiny family—I had thirty of them. Drago, my red-faced uncle, a fine singer, who very soon afterward would die in a drunken bout of a massive heart attack, slipped me a glass of wine and winked, conveying it all to me. The wine was sweet, terribly sweet, like one of those Kosher wines, Menshewitz. I drank the glass, and felt all the worse for it, and decided I wouldn't make such a mistake again. I wondered why wine was such a standard element in weddings, why even Jesus turned water into wine for a wedding? Did he drink at the wedding, and how much? It seemed at Mrvica's wedding, the wine disappeared, and people drank Seltzer water in the end. "I am glad, I am glad, I am glad," sang Cream. So this is it, this is the joy that awaits you, miserable weddings and communist party meetings, I thought, conversing with my alienated self, and thought more, get me out of here. And guess what, I am not out of here, and I am sort of glad for it, actually–very glad.

WINO

Before coming to America, in 1976, I had to undergo a little test, TESL, which reminded me of Tesla, but it stood for Test of English as a Second Language. My preparation was pretty iffy: The town in which I grew up was divided along many lines: believers and non-believers, communists and anti-communists, Serbs and Croats (and Czechs). These were all superficial divisions. The really deep and substantial one was between alcoholics and non-alcoholics. I was informed early on that I belonged to the non-alcoholic camp. My father, mother, and siblings—none of them drank. It was a little different with my uncles, one of whom fell off a barn after drinking plum brandy and broke his neck, and another kept a vineyard and was always flush faced, quiet, and jovial, selling suits in the center store. In late adolescence, I didn't drink at all, and I abhorred some of my friends who did. I heard they got together, drank beer and brandy, and passed out. Others went to village fairs, had fistfights and got drunk and had sex with village maidens in haystacks. Most of these were amateur drunks. A friend of mine, a few years older than me, informed me that alcoholism was a disease, first defined as such, coincidentally, in 1956, my birth year in the United States. Previously, alcoholism was a phenomenon, and now a disease. Pop (name of my friend) explained to me that there were all sorts of alcoholics, such as rakijasi (brandy drinkers), pivasi (beer drunks), and the worst of all winos (vinasi). Something in wine made these people hooked and incurable. I listened to Pop, with my mouth open. I didn't know any winos. Oh, you can recognize them easily, said Pop. They dehydrate, so when you see a man drink several glasses of water in the morning, you might look for the correlation of wine in the evening and the water in the morning. Nobody needs to drink water in the morning except alcoholics, he claimed.

However, winos were not all that bad, it turned out. Namely, when I needed to visit Belgrade to take the TESL (Teaching English as a Second Language) so I could apply to American colleges, I said to Pop, I can't afford a hotel in our capital. Do you know where I could crash for the night preceding my test? No problem, answered Pop. I know a wino who has a little house in Zemun, just outside of Belgrade, with excellent bus links to the center. How do I get in touch with him? I go to the post office and dial him? Oh no, he's always home. I'll give you the address. Just go there, bang on the door, as he's hard of hearing, and say you are Pop's friend, and give him a one liter bottle of red wine. You'll be his best friend right away. And you can sleep over. Now, maybe he'll be in a good phase, maybe not. His father is an officer, so he's protected, but still, now and then the police, who hate winos like him, come over and slap him. For a while they came every morning and woke him up by slapping his face and kicking him.

I followed Pop's instructions. It was a snowy and windy day in February. I came to a triangular square, found the little house, checked it out, finding that most of the windows were shattered, and then banged on the door. Mishko opened the door, tall, disheveled, with somewhat purple undersides to his eyes. I presented myself, and he laughed, Josip, like Tito. You must be Croatian? As though everybody loves Tito in Serbia. Nobody names children after him. Oh, and what do I see, a bottle of red. Yes, I replied, Plavac from Peljesac, Zinfandel from the Peljesac peninsula. Pop says I can spend the night here—I have to take tests at the American Embassy tomorrow. At the American Embassy!

By all means. We sat down and lit a petroleum lamp. I haven't paid the electric in a year, so the city has cut me off. The petrol fumes and smoke drifted, while he popped the bottle open and drank straight from it for a long while, finishing half of it. Good, now we can talk, he said. If you are tired, you can go right to bed, and cover yourself with that down cover.

I shivered as the snow blew through the windows into the room and the wind whistled over the shards of glass. Mishko walked to the cupboard, yanked a glass door open, and took out a handgun. Do you want to check it out? he asked. No, I am fine here, I said. It's really cold; I don't want to leave the bed. Fine, he said. It's an interesting gadget. My grandfather had a quarrel one day with my grandma. She was in bed just where you are, in the same bed, at midnight, like now, it's midnight, isn't it?—we haven't changed the furniture here since World War One, and he shot her. Yes, my friend, he killed my sweet grandma right there, with three bullets.

He started sobbing, and threw the handgun on the floor. He drank more wine, the snow blew through the cracked windows, and I shivered. Would you like a sip? Mishko asked. We need more wine, this is such damned good Croatian wine. No, thank you, I replied. Somehow, at that point I passed out and slept. Maybe the secondary lows affected me?

I woke up at dawn, found Mishko asleep in the armchair, covered by a large green officer's overcoat, with a couple of shoulder stripes, probably his grandfather's from World War One, and I walked out into the biting wind, and I stepped on the bus, and soon, I was at the American embassy. The administrators all smiled, displaying their enviably white teeth, and gave me a B2 pencil, to shade the ovals of the correct answers. They all drank water and I eyed them suspiciously.

BIBLE QUIZ

When I studied at Yale Divinity School, my student aid work alternated between working for a Congregationalist Church and for a half-way house for the criminally insane, recovering alcoholics, and other drug addicts. I had a degree in psychology, so I seemed well suited for the job. On one occasion, Jeff, a tall and powerful lad who was recovering from marijuana possession and a couple of muggings, asked me whether it would be all right if he went out into the street to the convenience store to buy a pack of cigarettes. I'll be right back.

No problem, I said. Just make sure not to mug anybody on the way.

He came back in half an hour, and soon after him, a couple of cops showed up, and asked for Jeff. True enough, he did go to the convenience store, but he also mugged someone and stole his wallet. So they took him away to spend a night in jail.

The director was upset with me. She said, You were not supposed to let him go. I missed the orientation, I didn't know. Of course I am sorry. But you know, it's just across the street. And he's recovered, he's on meds, very calm and all that. This is altogether very surprising.

Well, you can see how calm he is. He is just dangerous. I don't think he's coming back.

And my permissiveness didn't work all that well at the First United Church of Christ either. It was a congregationalist church, liberal, close to Unitarian, and it was also very rich. I was supposed to deliver a morning sermon once, and at that time I had stage fright, and to conquer it, I had a glass of vodka. Generally, I have no use for vodka—it has hardly any taste—but I used it medicinally as a tranquilizer. So empowered, I gave my inspired sermon, with a modest proposal. To go out and pleasantly surprise beggars in the streets by giving them all the cash reserves each member of the congregation had. Jesus would be proud of you if you gave, let's say, half a million dollars to a homeless bum.

The minister took me aside later and said that many people found my sermon offensive, or at any rate, not serious.

What's not serious about it? Haven't you read the New Testament? The young man asked Jesus, What more should I do to be saved? And Jesus answered, Give all your wealth to the poor…

The youth group went to the lakes in Western Connecticut near Storrs. Revered Willard and I led the group. We were nicely situated, in a beautiful huge log cabin at the lakeside. I taught the 12-year-olds how to play ping-pong and chess, but there was still too much time left in the day, and I proposed to run a Bible quiz. Revered Willard thought that was a brilliant idea. But the kids looked bored. What fun is that? They complained.

Tell you what. I have a bottle of red wine, and it will be like a holy communion. Whoever gives a correct answer gets a sip.

A sip? Why not a gulp? asked a precocious kid.

Fine, you can have a gulp if you answer some of these questions correctly.

Which patriarch had wrestled an angel of God and thereupon changed his name to Israel?

What city did Jonah want to see completely destroyed although his mission was to save it?

Did Moses have a bad temper? Why wasn't Moses allowed to enter the Promised Land?

Someone always got the right answer, and the quiz was a hit. The kids finished the bottle and they were loving the Bible. I was a good teacher.

When the minister found out, he was furious. You know, the kids will tell the parents, and we will both be in trouble. Why did you do it?

I didn't do anything wrong. I got them interested in the Bible. And you know, in many churches, the Holy Communion is conducted with real bread and real wine. For example, in my church in Daruvar, Croatia, it was done like that. (I thought about it, and it seemed to have been done like that for only a month before reverting to red grape-juice.)

Yeah, my friend, but this is America. You know if you didn't have this excuse, I am only a foreigner, what do you expect of me? I'd fire you right away. But now I will present the case as a loose European that does not understand American culture. OK? But don't do it again, is that clear?

I've never conducted another biblical quiz.

FREEDOM WINE

In 2003, when France disagreed with American Foreign Policy, American patriots shunned everything French, and French became a dirty adjective. In a few red parts of the country, French fries became Freedom fries. I don't know what happened to the French kiss—maybe it became Freedom kiss, or maybe they no longer kissed in the red states. At the time, I lived near State College in Central Pennsylvania, a region described as Alabama between Philadelphia and Pittsburgh, a rather reddish part of the state, blushingly so. Sometimes it was embarrassing to be from there and to pass all the NRA signs, and such signs as "We Have Worms. *First Iraq then Chirac.*" When France was shunned there was one good result. A wine store on North Atherton in State College slashed the price of a Bordeaux-supérieur from twenty to seven a bottle, and I got an additional ten percent off as I bought a case of the wine—actually three. Nobody was buying French at the store, so this was a desperate way to move the product, which agreed with me and my despair. I organized a Freedom party, Liberté Égalité etc. Many friends and acquaintances came to the party in our house on a ridge, in Warriors Mark, up a very unfriendly lane, full of rocks and bumps. We were surrounded by a forest, and bears occasionally visited our yard, especially during the raspberry season. Now some people came from far away for this party—a Belgrade chess player and gambler drove from Troy, New York at eighty-five miles an hour without getting a ticket; my niece, who studied philosophy, and her brooding fiancé from Philadelphia; Olga, a Byelo-Russian ex-wife of the son of a former Prime Minister of France came with her son Sasha from Pittsburgh. I poured glasses of liberty wine to all the guests. My wife had procured a set of large wine glasses so that each one accommodated half a bottle. Almost everybody had refills. We melted Brie and smeared it over split baguettes, and everybody ate. We listened to French chansons, Aznavour, and Piaf. The wine was excellent, lots of Wine Spectator adjectives could be applied. Everybody seemed to be in an excellent mood, and nobody vomited at the end of the evening. The crates in which the wines came were pretty, and we used them as beds for our cats for months afterwards, and as vinyl record containers, filled with Johnny Cash and other freedom lovers.

STEPHEN'S VINTAGE

My son and I visited Stephen, my friend who ran an art colony on an island in Maine, in Bedford, New York, and drove down the lane to his refurbished red farmhouse. We stepped on huge floor tiles, each one about four square feet, a bit uneven, thick, foot worn to a polish, reminding me of churches in Europe.

Stephen, these tiles are impressive, I said.

They better be, he said. I bought a whole damned monastery in France to get the tiles.

Really, you are crazy.

I had the monastery floor taken apart and shipped to me. I still have a lot of stones I'll use somehow.

How did you find the monastery?

On eBay.

You could have just as well bought hundreds of bottles of Bordeaux.

I could have but these tiles are more solid. By the way, it's fantastic to see you, he said. Let's have some special wine for the occasion. You know, I have this wine cellar that I inherited from one of my friends, a large brewing company heir, who died in Munich. He left millions to his various wives and lovers, and I was his will executor, and he left me just 300 bottles of damned fine French wines, which are probably past their prime, but each one, a minimum of 500 bucks. I haven't had any yet. Would you mind splitting a bottle?

Yes, I would mind, I said. Why didn't he drink them up before he died?

He was a sick man, an alcoholic. Strange karma, isn't it, for a beer mogul. He could drink only vodka or gin. He needed an immediate alcoholic surge. Wine was too slow for him. The heritage of wine was wasted on him. After his death, his autopsy showed that his brain had shrunk to the size of an average apple.

OK, let's not think about apples, I said, but grapes, and let's drink. The drive was hell.

So we drank a bottle, and it was all right. I forgot its name. Maybe we should have decanted it. Then we drank a bottle of wine I got from a friend of mine, a wine distributor, an Englishman—a Californian merlot, Fess Parker (Dave Crockett actor turned winemaker), which would sell in the range of forty, or so, and it was much tastier somehow than the dusty and sour old French wine. My son played the cello, a Chopin piece, soulfully, and I wondered why the hell he was so abused to become a virtuoso. He reminded me of the anecdote from Diogenes Laertius, which goes approximately like this—Diogenes listened to a young man play the lyra, and the more he played, the sadder Diogenes was, and he started weeping. What's wrong, the host said, doesn't he play beautifully? Yes, he does. The more he plays, the more I realize how much time the poor lad has spent practicing. I mourn for all that time he wasted. I felt a bit like that for my son, but then I thought, maybe the fucking French wine was making me sentimental and irrational.

Next time I visited Stephen, I said, How is your cellar holding up?

Better than it should, he replied.

How so?

I forgot the code and my wife is hiding it from me. She wants me to quit drinking. So I have kind of quit. And also, she doesn't understand that wine is not like a museum. Wine improves for a while and then gets worse, and museums get better and better with age. We should drink it all for a month and have a festival of silliness, but instead it will be really corked and foul. But what do I care? I can just imagine how the wine is doing in a vault. It's like Italian liras after the introduction of the Euro. They were still good for a year and you could exchange them, and now, they are just pretty things to put on the wall. And not even all that pretty. The French francs are prettier and so are the Dutch guilders. But they are all now worthless.

PERSONAL HISTORY OF BEER

My first taste of beer, like of coffee, was so disgusting that I never imagined that I would actually like it later on. When I was twelve, my mother worked in the garden on a hot summer day and asked me to help her. We were both sweating and she said, Son, there's only one thing that works to cool you off on a day like this. Beer. Go to the corner store and buy two half-liter beers. I was a bit surprised as my mother was a strict Baptist, but I guess beer didn't count as alcohol. After all, ninety-five percent of it was not alcohol. And when I had a taste of it, I said, This is awful, so bitter. Maybe, she said, but have a couple more sips, and you will cool off. So it's medicinal?

After that, I contemptuously watched the elderly drunks, both fat and thin, who sat all over the town of Daruvar and drank beer all day long. Until then, I was kind of intrigued, thinking there must be something good in beer, but now, I looked at them with astonishment. So, this is what they live for, to drink that bitter shit?

I swore I would never drink it again. Anyhow, ten years later, at the age of twenty-two, I had just arrived in Eindhoven, after flying from JFK to Amsterdam, from where I would hitchhike to Stuttgart, where my sister lived. When I walked into a supermarket in Eindhoven, I laughed at three young men who had filled their cart with Grolsches. You are getting nothing else but just beer? I asked. What else do we need? Bier ist Nahrung, said one guy, a tall

German. This is a complete set of groceries for the night, said an Englishman. Anyway, you are welcome to join us. I was impressed by the patented bottles which opened with a pop, and somehow, because I was hungry and thirsty, the beer immediately tasted good, scratching my throat amiably. And so we drank Grolsch all night, and covered the history of Europe since Franco-Prussian wars, and when the German was completely drunk, he wept because it was so damned embarrassing to be German.

In the morning, not feeling all that great, I hitchhiked to Koeln, and there, hopped on a train to Stuttgart, traveling without a fare, mostly in bathrooms, because, fuck you Germans, I owe you nothing. I was caught in Mannheim and kicked off the train. Anyway, in Stuttgart I got further education in beer drinking—my brother-in-law introduced me to Hefeweizen, wheat beer—and continued to be educated about the Czech Republic, when I went to the pub where Bohumil Hrabal usually drank. He wasn't there, but his beer was—people said, any minute now, he'll be here. And I understood how he could spend every evening drinking that shit. It was bitter and good! The education continued in Croatia, in my hometown, which had a large brewery, Staro Cesko Pivo, Old Czech beer, more or less the same thing which I so hated as a 12-year-old, but enjoyed now. My sister-in-law became the chief accountant of the brewery, and the Baptist church deacon, and as a Czech patriot, bought shares in the company. Usually, he fought against alcoholism in the church, but beer was something else, not all that bad, and yes, it was Czech, some old formula.

The best beer around that time, I had two years later in a monastery in Ziegelhausen, Benediktinerabtei, north of Heidelberg, overlooking the river Neckar. I stayed in the monastery for a month to read the entire Bible in the Luther translation in German. My reward was that every evening I would get a pint of ale that the monks made right there, and it came from large rotting oak barrels, which enhanced the flavor. After Gregorian chants, prayers, and then a couple of half-liters, the monks were pretty close to God.

After European beer, it was hard to adjust to Budweiser and some other watery American beer. In Germany, I had become a beer snob. Now and then, I needed to go back to Europe, as a beer exile form North America. But then, upon moving to New York City, I had New Amsterdam, which proved to be an excellent beer, made in small quantities. It was expensive. And pretty soon, microbrews sprung up all over. I think the first one I visited was in Berkeley, California, in 1991. It was amazing—strong, with substance, body, texture, fresh yeast, hoppy. It was better than the English ales I had in pubs. I read somewhere that now in the States, one microbrewery per day is the rate of new breweries opening up.

Montreal. When I moved here, I had friends who liked to meet at Copa (a bar named after Copocabana) and they drank local beer, Boréale, produced in large enough quantities not to be considered a microbrew. But then I discovered a microbrew pub, Dieu du Ciel, on Laurier. It's a small brew pub, with a dozen micro brews on the menu every day. Alcohol content varies between four percent to ten percent. After a couple of pints, by seven, many people become drunk, and the place becomes extremely loud. I don't know why it is that people who drink become louder and louder. Anyhow, the beer there, I realized, tasted much better than the English ales I recently had in London, but perhaps, that is partly to do with the alcohol content? Some of the ales had three point five alcohol content, basically like American Budweiser. Sure, they taste good but not sharp and strong. At a Lancaster beer pub, I was impressed at the pricing. Regardless of the quality or fame of the ale, the price was a mathematical formula of alcohol percentage. The more alcohol, the more you pay for the brew. Basically, they treat beer as an indifferent medium through which the essential thing, alcohol, is delivered. The rest is packaging. That struck me as both rational and crude.

The advantage of weak beer is that you can't get drunk quickly and easily, and so a friend of mine, John, when he's sick of hangovers, drinks only beer and he claims he is on the wagon. I learnt that from Paul Newman, he told me. After drinking a lot of bourbon as a young man, Newman quit, and for forty years, he had a six-pack of beer every night. He considered that he was practically a teetotaler.

Yes, it seems like a nice principle, but with the new microbrews it might not keep you out of trouble. In my neighborhood, Vices and Versa, on St. Laurent, near the arches of Little Italy, usually sells around thirty different beers. I go for the bitter ones. The best combination is a high octane IPA. At nine percent alcohol content, it's as strong as some of the German Rieslings, and the notion that it's only beer can be perilous.

Anyway, I am pleased with my neighborhood just north of Bernard because it has Italians who make the best coffee in the Province of Quebec (macchiato nearly as good as in Milan), and I'll admit it: because of the fantastic microbrewery, Helm, on Bernard. Now I understand Hegel—not so much his philosophy as his life-style. When looking for a university position, he deemed whether it was worthwhile to accept it based on the quality of the local brew as he had to have his half-liter (or two) every afternoon.

THE THIRD ROUND

After the wars had ended in Croatia, I ran into a man I hadn't expected to see alive in my hometown, Daruvar, in Western Slavonia: an old Serbian policeman, a convicted murderer who had killed a Croatian drunk at a village tavern two decades before the war. I had distilled the man into a minor character in a chapter of my novel, which was translated into Croatian. A young man, Stanisa, had come to my book presentation in Daruvar several years earlier and asked, You wrote about my dad, didn't you, you put him into a book? I'd love to have a copy. I was sure Stanisa was speaking about the policeman. (Later, I figured out his father was a different cop, who had tracked me down—I was around ten—for swiping an American flag off a black Mercedes in front of our courthouse. I decorated our empty sheep stall in the backyard with the silky flag—we were too close to the center of town to be allowed to keep animals, by the new ordinance—and the cop, who had a cleft chin like Kirk Douglas, showed up, took the flag, and reprimanded me, but it was clear he wouldn't hit me as, for example, a forester once had.)

After the murder, Badzo (nickname for *Boss* in Serbian) continued to be a threat, having served only a three-year sentence. He worked as a guard at the hot springs spa pool at the new hotel. The spa was two thousand-years-old, Aqua Balissae in the Roman Empire. As kids, we often found small Roman coins in the mud in the park and near the brick factory, in the green clay. Whenever I visited Daruvar, I liked to swim at midnight in the steaming water, but Badzo did his rounds, and sometimes I ducked into the water and waited for him to pass by. He walked around like a caricature of a Western cowboy, with a protruding stomach, and hands slung down wide, as though ready to draw a gun, but he was not allowed to carry a gun, though in our town that didn't mean much.

I had heard that during the war, instead of joining the Serbian forces in the hills, he stayed in town. He volunteered to join the Croatian forces, but nobody trusted him. A couple of men beat him in the park, nearly to death. That's one version I heard. Another is that at the beginning of the war, Croatian right-wing paramilitary kept him a prisoner in a dark basement on bread and water, along with several other local Serbs, to prevent them from leaving, and his family didn't know where he was. He may have been treated cruelly.

A friend of mine, a bass player, Skala, while in the new Croatian army uniform, had run into Badzo on the bridge over the river Toplica, and he aimed his rifle at Badzo, and said, Stoj! (*Stop*).

Badzo said, What, you are going to shoot me? Just like that?

Yes.

But I have nothing, no weapons, and you have, what is it? A Kalashnikov?

Nice balance of power, don't you think? You've abused it all your life. Don't move, hands up.

Please don't shoot. What have I ever done to you?

You were an ugly sight, spoiled my field of vision. You've fucked around enough, it's all over for you.

If you let me live, I will buy you beer whenever I see you in town.

Well, you're in hiding, what if you don't see me? A bad deal for me. I visualized this for years. This is my wish fulfilled. I want you dead.

Just give me a call, and I will come out and get you some Old Czech beer. How about a couple right now?

Okay. It is hot.

And they went to the nearest tavern at the farmers' market and drank a few, and Badzo lived on. Afterward, he retreated into his apartment. He developed a heart murmur.

Anyhow, almost twenty-five years later, when I saw Badzo near the center of Daruvar, I thought, This could be a mutually unpleasant encounter. He looked into my eyes, I into his, and the recognition was immediate, no words necessary, but nevertheless, we said good day to each other simultaneously. His hair was still black, greasy, and he had a double chin, small glistening eyes, and thick arched eyebrows. We stood in front of Rock Café, the fulfillment of my childhood friend Željac's DJ dreams; he had founded the café a couple of years earlier. Badzo and I shook hands, and I said, How about a glass of red?

You are a mind reader, he said. But I'm broke.

Don't worry. That's why there are Americans. My treat.

We sat down, and I kept buying him glasses of red.

Good wine, he said. Now, even local red wine is good. They used to make only good Riesling, but maybe the climate has changed, and the reds are excellent.

Željac seemed puzzled by the company. I used to have Afro-style hair, and in the early seventies people called me Jimi after Hendrix. I knew Željac admired me, but that I would hang out with an antithesis of hip, a former regime cop, increased the size of his pupils. Well, life was a little more complex than any of us knew or know. Meanwhile, Željac played Led Zeppelin's "Whole Lotta Love" ironically. He'd saved for a long time to get a permit for this café, and now he served the best macchiatos around. He still had long blond hair, although he was over fifty. I don't know many people rock music has kept young, but it preserved him, as though no time had passed and no wars had taken place. He complained that he had to pay too much tax—there was so little economy in town that the county offices squeezed the last drop of cash out of anybody who had anything resembling an enterprise.

Badzo said, Doctors tell me I shouldn't do this, but look, I am seventy-five, and all this is a bonus. I've learned a lot. And my life is almost over. How old are you?

Fifty-nine.

Okay, sixty. We are through with it all. We don't have to worry about sex, wars, death ...

Death, we must worry about.

No, it's guaranteed.

I thought you would have gone to Belgrade.

I am a local patriot. For me, homeland is the square kilometer where I have lived most of my life. You can only get me out of here dead. I've bought my gravesite, I'm all set, just a kilometer up the hill. So you probably can't even get me out of here dead. Alive has failed; many people have tried to boot me out of here.

Didn't you want Greater Serbia?

Let's not talk about that, my friend. Perhaps, if it came here, but that's why I wanted it to be Greater, so I wouldn't have to travel there. I hate travel. Plus, I can't afford it. I don't think I could buy bus fare to Belgrade now. And I don't want to see it. Good luck to them over there. But they fucked up, with their aggression and idiocy.

Serves them right. Do you remember how we played a chess game poolside almost fifty years ago?

Yes, you exchanged your queen for two rooks, which should have been a great deal, but then you got mated.

Amazing, you deserve one more glass of wine for this. (I'd been arrogant, thought he was a stupid cop, and I was nervous, surrounded by a few other cops in black Speedos, who smoked and laughed at the game, rooting for me to beat Badzo. But he was a solid player, obviously smarter than I gave him credit for. Still, I think stage fright contributed to my loss, but no matter; he was smart.)

He drank more, grew redder. There was a lot we didn't talk about. There was a lot we wouldn't talk about. I had wondered if he'd mind me for using him in my novel. Would he like to revisit the case? Of course not. I didn't know the details of his crime, just the raw fact. Who knows how it went, what insults were exchanged, supposedly along ethnic lines, Croat-Serb. Maybe he hadn't read the passages, maybe he had and didn't care, maybe he had and liked what I made of it. In my novel he was a beer guzzler with a beer gut, and I wrote about that while drinking red wine, and lo and behold, he was a wino like me. And not only that, he was a smart conversationalist. Maybe his walking like a caricature of John Wayne was an expression of his sense of humor. How he survived the encounter with Skala also showed quick thinking and a sense of humor. I marveled at how he rebuilt his life after the terrible crime. A murder may take thirty seconds of your life, but once a murderer, always a murderer, unlike, say, a thief. If you don't steal again, you are no longer a thief. How do you redeem yourself after a murder? This man may have succeeded. Maybe he'd even saved lives. And he'd suffered probably more than I could guess. I certainly couldn't judge him after all these years.

Željac played some blues, John Mayall, and stared out into the street. Not enough customers. Maybe Badzo and I didn't present an inviting sight. Badzo drank red wine, I drank cappuccino, since I was under the illusion that I was on the wagon, and so we sat. It amazed me that I was talking to a character from my novel, as he'd become more of that in my imagination than the actual man in front of me.

I got him one more glass, and we shook hands, and he seemed overjoyed, blessed: to him I may have represented a chimerical past, somebody from an old era, when the world was better, still talking to him. The town had changed in the war. Many Serbs left, some Croats too. Bosnian refugees moved in. The town population was declining, many houses were for sale, the old factories had died. Still, some people stayed staunchly on, resisting the temptation to emigrate somewhere better. Such as my friend Boris, my older brother, and a few other people, including Skala.

Later that night, a rock band played at Željac's café. The place was crowded, lively (or rather deadly, as people still smoked indoors in cafés despite weak efforts by the government to outlaw it). I was dizzy from smoke, noise, time travel; Boris was drinking Staročesko—that's the name of the Old Czech beer, one of the oldest lineage beers in the former Yugoslavia, a tribute to the large Czech minority in town. Skala stopped by. He was mostly Czech but for some reason a rabid Croat in the war, perhaps, because of a sense of justice, as he hated the Serbian aggression and the Milošević regime. I hadn't seen him in a few years. Instead of getting a pension as a war veteran, he had no income; he had grown thinner, grayer, but not even he had lost his hair; it had turned white, even his sparse, two-week-old goatee was gray. What was it about these men that they didn't grow bald, I wondered. Maybe the balding types like me emigrated and the solid-hair types stayed. Skala used to harass me when I visited before and during the war, saying that I was a Mason working against Croatia. And so I didn't like to talk to him, and even now I was wary he'd have one of his tirades, but no, he sat humbly, and I realized he'd love a beer so I got him a couple.

He was happy and said it was great to see me; he'd even forgive the bass player for being out of tune. He was proud of his perfect pitch and couldn't get along with any bands, since he constantly pestered everybody for being out of tune, but playing in bands used to be his source of income, and now he'd just sold his father's apartment for next to nothing and was running out of money.

A year later I was visiting the town again, and Rock Café was gone; now it was a small store selling plumbing supplies. I asked my friend Boris what happened to the café.

He said, Well, Željac missed rent payments for three months, and they kicked him out without a warning.

And how about Badzo? I asked. Do you see him?

No, he's ill. That doesn't mean he wouldn't have a glass with you if you ran into him. I think he may be dying, may be dead already, I'm not sure, I don't really keep up. You could ask his sons or his wife.

I didn't know he had sons.

Yeah, he's a real family man.

How about Skala?

Boris said, He had one of his episodes, so he was institutionalized for a couple of months, and now he is heavily medicated, too heavily. He's a zombie, has no will, isn't allowed to have a drink, and lives in the house for social cases. He gets one hundred kunas (sixteen dollars) a month for coffee and eats at a private home, mostly rice, beans, bread, apples. His caretakers beat him if he comes home late or smells of cigarettes.

So, nobody is better than before?

Nobody, he said. Are you?

DAMIR

The times which I dreaded have come: I have to think whether I have more friends above the ground or in the ground. My childhood friend, Damir Horvat Zacskai, has just died in Daruvar. *Sreli smo se sa desetak godina jer smo obojica bili ponosni na nas hrapavi I glasni kronicni bronchitis. On bi stao na jedno brdo pored skole, I hroptao sto glasnije je mogao, I morao sam priznati da bolje hropce I da jace kaslje od mene.* He used his illness to drive his teachers crazy: he coughed whenever they wanted to make a point, and their voices couldn't compete with his cough.

He loved to read books and discovered Bruno Traven, *The Treasures of Sierra Madre* and *Death Ship*. On *Death Ship* people drank rum, so, as his father was a bar owner, Damir managed to get a bottle of rum. Instead of going to church for New Year's Eve, he visited me and we listened to the Rolling Stones and Jimi Hendrix, and for some reason the electricity went out. While fixing the fuses, I managed to screw them all up and anyhow, we passed out from rum. It was probably a lucky thing the electrical system failed as we could have got electrocuted. My mother was shocked to find the house all dark and rank from our vomit and after that, she didn't want to see him at our house, but Damir was way too cultured to keep him out.

My brother Ivo at the time played the classical guitar and gave Damir lessons. Pretty soon they got the idea that we should have a rock band, something like Cream, but without drums, for the time being. Damir helped his father in running the bar, Daruvarski podrum, and got paid for being abused for childhood labor. My mother paid Ivo and me for helping her make wooden shoes. I also earned money by collecting chamomile tea in the fields around Daruvar, and I collected bushels of cherries from our huge garden and sold them to the cooperative on the next block. We managed to save enough money to buy good amplifiers, have bass and lead guitar hand-made in Zagreb. I played the violin, and wanted to be like the violinist in Vanilla Fudge. We were all soloists, improvising, without a central melody to work with. Nobody wanted to keep the rhythm for the others. Damir gave us a name: Fresh Factual Emancipation. We subscribed to the Melody Maker, and I was more interested in reading the rock journal than in playing. I papered our living room in Melody Maker pages. The garage/basement where we practiced flooded that year, and neighbors complained about the noise, of course. I actually feared that we might become a real band which would mean concerts on stage, and I had stage fright. Ivo became interested in Pendercki's electronic music, and he wanted our fusion to include classical experimentation. He read Adorno's music theory and we ended up philosophizing rather than playing. Maybe we would have become a rock band, but Damir then, to become a better bass player, went to Zagreb and studied the cello at a high-school music school. I gave Damir a present for his trip. Namely, my brother Vlado, as a doctor, got lots of bottles of plum brandy and piglets from the Serbian peasants around Daruvar. Usually the plum brandy was top-notch—some of it was from the same batch that was given to colonels and generals of JNA. I stole a bottle from my brother's basement (he paid no attention as he didn't drink at all and neither did I), and Damir shared it with five to six other lads from his music school and they all got terribly ill and some had to be treated in the ER. I wrote about that incident, a segment of a story, "Rock: Twenty Years After," which I published in the Threepenny

Review. Damir was furious and said he could retaliate and write disgraceful things about me too.

I saw Damir last December, and while we listened to lots of jazz and blues, he almost wept about how we failed to become a rock band, Fresh Factual Emancipation. I said, But look, even how you chose the name for the band showed you were a poet. You chose well. He said, It's all Ivo's fault. I said, You know, he had an offer from Crveni Koralji to join them. And he said, I know that, but they were not a serious band. We played wonderful fusion. It kills me we lost all the recordings and have only memories left.

I said, Damir, it seems I will write a series of profiles for Jutarnji List, would it be OK if I wrote about you, and he said, Yes, no problem. And you can say whatever you want because I might be dead by the time you publish the profile. Oh, no, I said, we won't take decades to publish it, maybe in a couple of months. Even so, he said, I'll be dead by then.

He complained that night about his health, stomach aches, and ate his favorite beans with spicy Hungarian sausages, at two in the morning, at the end of my visit. Later, I asked Tony Hnojcik, our mutual friend, who has also died in the meantime. Listen, what's up with Damir? He's talking about dying. Tony answered, he's fine. He just hopes to get to a hospital to get some affection from the nurses.

Anyhow, Damir had years ago bought an old-style one-floor house in Daruvar, and kept a whole wing of it for his books and records. Every night he listened to fine music and read books, poetry, novels. He remained faithful to the life-style of early youth. He loved English, read Joyce, and brought the same kind of neologism inventiveness into his Croatian. He complained that since he lived in the provinces and not in Zagreb, he would never be recognized. I do think he could have become famous and maybe still will be—if he had moved in literary circles of influence. He has published, however, several books of poems, and individual poems in Quorum and other influential magazines. Perhaps he had no sense of judging which of his poems were top notch and which weren't, and even within the same poem he could create sublime lines and slip ... something that could have been corrected by good editing.

Although Hungarian to a large extent, he was a Croatian patriot, and I thought for fifteen years, during the war and shortly after it, the patriotism made his poetry too sentimental and predictable. Later, Croatian politics and economy impoverished the region, and his business of selling books, new and used all over Slavonia, especially the villages, barely sustained him. Perhaps the fact that the promised land, Free Croatia, didn't translate into a better life for him tempered his patriotism, and he wrote brilliantly again and regained his sense of irony and humor. He could strike a chord, really surprise you with his word choices and coinages. He savored words and rhythms and linguistic melodies, the way he savored his fish paprikash and plum brandy. In many ways he was a linguistic genius, playful and inventive.

And I must say, I admire the stability of him remaining a Daruvar Canin. It used to be an art form: how to leave your provincial town. Now it's an art form: how to stay. In the last three decades, more people left than remained. Nearly everybody from our generation left, and very few people knew how to stay, and so it was a pleasure, upon visiting to find someone from my youth, still in town, and still doing the same things as fifty years ago, still reading beautiful books, listening to wonderful music, and talking eagerly and enthusiastically, till late at night. Well, I am talking to him right now, deep into the night.

TONI THE WAR PHOTOGRAPHER

War is the King of us all, said Heraclites. That certainly applies to Toni Hnojcik, my old friend and photographer, who had done a lot of art photography featuring flowers and white horses from Lipik (named after Lipizzaner, one of the breeding grounds for the Hapsburgs) and charming young women, but in the war, he found his subject. He went to the front lines when the war in Croatia broke out in 1991, and beyond them, and took pictures of the dead, the wounded, and also of the bored soldiers, destruction, abandoned farms, roaming master-less animals. He suddenly became an artist and transcended his somewhat kitsch initial impulses. He was a friend, and no, I don't want to be a pig-critic, but the war elevated his vision, which had been too rosy and pretty before it. He became a War Photographer on a mission. He was intrepid, and his work became urgent, important, exciting. And as a Czech, he had no reason to take sides between the Croats and the Serbs, but he did hate the aggressors, who at the time were the generals from Serbia, and the local Serbian militants.

That was almost a surprise. He was a hippy, with long hair, leather jackets, and motorcycles, a bit of a hell's angel, and a pacifist. I don't remember him entering any physical fights—he negotiated all the conflicts with humor, compromise, and everybody caught a bit of his good mood. His superior intelligence and temperament and courage got him through a lot.

He should have become famous for his photographs. Some of them ended up in the New York Times, International Herald Tribune, and other famous places, but usually his name was not there. His were among the first war pictures from the Balkans in the 90's to show up internationally.

My brother Vlado claims that the first missile in the war was fired into his room at the Pakrac Hospital in Western Slavonia, Croatia. He was dozing off in his chair, on duty as an emergency ophthalmologist, rather than in his bed. Suddenly, the glass shattered and a missile landed in his bed. It struck his pillows and didn't go off. The pillow, and inches, saved his life. He ran out of the room, and the bomb never went off. Anyhow, very soon afterward, Toni was there, taking pictures of the shattered hospital, which according to the Yugoslav Federal army hosted renegade Croatian police. Toni sold the photos to journalists at the Hotel Intercontinental in Zagreb—many of them stayed at the bar drinking Jack Daniels. They'd buy a photo from him for 100 dollars, and he'd go out into the field and bring a new harvest. That was before digital photography; he developed them in a darkroom.

He also worked as a photojournalist for several newspapers in Zagreb, Arena, Vecernji List. At the time everybody read newspapers, and he earned a good living. But after the war, although he should have gotten a medal for his work, he received no pension. He lived very poorly, so poorly that last year he couldn't afford to buy a bus ticket to attend his sister's funeral in Daruvar.

He reverted to the psychedelic vision of gauze clouds, tulip fields, and enhanced colors, as though on an acid trip. Another war would have saved him, but perhaps drinking froze him in an earlier stage of beauty ... thirst for beauty.

I ran into him at Tresnjevka Plac during my last visit to Zagreb in 2017, before a trip to Latvia, when I was suddenly and very justifiably worried about my blood chemistry. We had coffee and talked. He insisted on taking many photos of me, and I said, but it's too early in the day, I haven't shaved, and I am a bit hungover.

That's a natural condition. That's your character. You don't want to hide it. I must say that with age, your face shows more character than before.

OK, but please stop.

He took a couple more and said, Well, you never know when we'll see each other next. I haven't seen you in years. Maybe never?

You are right. Neither of us complains but it doesn't mean we are all right, I said.

The main thing is to avoid the doctors, he said.

Yes, I have avoided my brother doctor for a while, and others, and thought that guaranteed good health.

I haven't seen any of them, or better to say, I haven't let any of them see me in a decade. But come on, between the two of us, we can't rely on a reunion, so let's make the best of it.

True enough.

He died suddenly of a massive heart attack. Age sixty-six. Three months later, I was diagnosed with prostate trouble. I did mind it that he smoked around me but so did everybody and I am sure that has nothing to do with my condition, but it may have killed him, never to have kicked off the cig habit.

The last time I had sat together with him was more than ten years ago. He ran into Boris and me in my childhood street of Mose Pijade (Jewish partisan) now renamed Ban Jelacica (a count who helped suppress the Hungarian revolution of 1848) in Daruvar, and said, Hey, Boys, I am gonna be a dad! My wife is at the hospital in Bjelovar about to give birth. I'll ride the motorbike in a bit, but let's first have a round of drinks to celebrate.

Will you be able to ride after that? I said.

I've had a lot of training. Come on, I don't see you that often, this is a double holiday.

So, we sat down at Gradska Kavana and had a few rounds of beer and whiskey. He was so happy that he never made it to the hospital. He got a call that he was a dad to a young son, and he said, I'd be, of course, just as happy to have a daughter. But this is great! I am a dad.

Aren't you supposed to go to the hospital? Come on, man, this is life.

Sure, I'll do that later, when I sober up.

When will that be?

Good point, one more round!

Anyway, I do believe he was a good dad. Not a great husband, so his wife divorced him. He invited Damir, me, and another guy home after the bar closed, and we kept drinking.

So, your wife is a veterinarian doctor, I said.

Yes, who else could put up with an animal like me? But maybe I am not enough of an animal, I don't know. She deserves better and more sex than what I can provide. Tell you what, let's see whether she's in the mood, we could all have sex with her right now. Maybe she will be satisfied. I'd love to see her happy.

He went to the bedroom and broached this idea to his wife. She came out with a stick and chased us all out into the yard. I don't remember much; I think we had drunk so much that we vomited.

Anyhow, I don't think that Toni spent much time at home. The war came on shortly afterwards, and he was always looking for action. It's a miracle he hadn't gotten injured or killed. Fifty-five journalists died covering the wars in Croatia and Bosnia.

While the war and alcohol wrecked his marriage, the war built his career for a while. Twenty-five years later, nobody seems to care much about the past war. The print journals have almost all vanished, and the pay for photographs has gone down.

Nevertheless, he kept up his good moods.

When my novel Fool's Day was published in Croatia, the cover art was Hnojcik's. That was the work of my editor at Algoritam. He said, Wait, aren't you and Toni childhood friends? I believe his work would bring some good spirit to your novel.

How could I disagree? A great idea.

I thought Kruno Lokotar, the editor, would get some war photography, but instead, he got a whirlwind of flowers, a vortex that was underground and interesting and a fitting image, despite my not being a flower guy.

By no means was Toni a naïve artist, but his obsession with beauty hindered him. Toni was trained in Prague at the school for film and photography as a member of the Czech minority of Daruvar. (Well, my grandmother had come from Prague, so technically, I could have claimed to be a member of the same community, and my nephew Damir, also a photographer, got an invitation from the same famous photo school with a scholarship, but he said, I am all right being local.) Surprisingly, Toni came back, but then why not? He was a photojournalist for the Jednota, a Czech weekly, covering Czech events, holidays, personalities, and so on. He was what we called a Frajer, or cool dude. Translation of Freier, not Friar. From the German. After all, this was a province of Austria-Hungary for several hundred years.

To go back a while, I had some reasons to resent Toni. While I was a repressed Baptist, not allowed to date, he at the age of seventeen rode motorcycles, looking like Mick Jagger, except better, and the girls were crazy about him. I admired the freedom Toni had, which I thought I would never have. Later, Toni admired me for dodging the Yugoslav Federal Army draft, going to the States, and coming back now and then. We were good friends after all, and I wish we had spent more time together. And we would have …

Now, in retrospect, it was thoroughly amazing to run into him before his death. I complained to him that our mutual friend D.

could have several cancers and wouldn't last, and he laughed, Oh, he just needs love. He thinks nurses can do it for him. I wouldn't worry about him.

He didn't say he would worry about the two of us. But there he is, or rather, isn't. I heard that cheerful Czech music was played at his funeral, and the eulogy said, Toni loved beer, women, and motorbikes. Probably in that order. It was a large funeral, a lot of beer flowed, and many women wept. Motorbike engines stayed quiet.

DARKENED VISION

Pavle, attracted to women who wore glasses, married Zora when she could still see. Through her glasses, her irises looked magnified, removed, and, even when dry, brilliantly tearful. Not that the glasses had been the key factor in his attraction to her, but they had enhanced her; she had looked dreamy and sensuous. Her dim vision had perhaps enhanced him as well; who knows whether she would have married him if she could have seen him in focus. Looking through her blue irises to the crystals of green and black, he dreamed. Her look grew dreamier and dreamier and steadier and steadier until it became clear that she was blind. He bought her a pair of black glasses as if preparing her for the eclipse of the sun.

Wherever he went, the black glasses hovered in his mind, and the eyes behind the glasses loomed accusingly, as if he had blinded her. It is not always true that the blind feel the seeing more than the seeing feel the blind—at least it wasn't in his case. He developed a sixth sense for her. Cutting wood miles away from her, he saw her sitting on the wooden steps in the sun, moving her ears and expanding her nostrils.

She sat on her steps, her ears moving like a hawk's wings in landing. She could hear Pavle's vehicle on its way home from a mile away, he was sure.

At home, she monitored his every motion, suspecting he would leave. When he opened the door, she asked, "And where now so late at night?" Most often she said nothing, and he felt the question all the more, "And where now so late at night?"

Late at night, out of their house came snoring that sounded like a saw cutting a knotty log of oak. Pavle was hiding in his snore from his wife's flesh. As he slept he felt her ears moving unhappily, and he would wake up and toss and turn in bed until he fell asleep again or lust took possession of him. He touched her and she embraced him like an octopus. To him it seemed she felt more than he ever could. A smile of knowledge floated around her lips, forming two spiraled dimples. He shook, as if to shrug off his skin, like a snake in the spring. Her limbs turned into electric eels. He shivered like prey whose strength was being conducted away. His revulsion ignited his marrow and returned to him his strength doubly. In heavy weightlessness, as if in water, they twisted around each other. Sensing the commotion of slimy marine wonders in the ocean underneath, he tried to swim to the surface, away from the maelstrom swallowing him into the underworld.

The carnal storms between them were rare. The oceanic horror stayed with him, concentrated in the image of the iris-less whites bulging beneath her black glasses. The mutilating, empty eyes watched him as his helper, a crimson peasant, lifted logs onto the platform of Pavle's vehicle, as Pavle pushed the logs onto a vertical motor-propelled saw.

Pavle worked accurately and rhythmically, as though regretting that not more skill was involved so that he could be proud of his handiwork. There was something encouragingly simple in the repetition of motions in work—the sensation of becoming mechanized and infallible. There was also something discouragingly simple, which bored him and prevented him from becoming a machine. As he pushed a log, the high-pitched sound of the disk saw grew lower and lower until it reached the midpoint of the wood—it was not clear which moaned more, the steel or the wood—and then higher and higher, to buzz freely when the wood slid off. His helper poured water over the saw, as if baptizing the steel, lest it overheat. During breaks, Pavle and his helper poured slivovitz over their throats, lest they overheat. As the helper tossed a mouthful of brandy from one cheek to the other, his face grew redder, his irises bluer, and his eyeballs whiter. He swore against the government. The government had collectivized his land, reducing him to bare hands no one but Pavle would hire. Old people sat in chairs and, under the pretext of entertainment, watched the work being done; now during the break they were ready to joke, but Pavle's mood quieted them. Pavle charged his services uniformly. Old and poor people he charged so little that he made no profit. He charged them like a judge who, despite the evidence that you committed the crime, pronounced a mild sentence on the account of your extenuating passions.

Having finished the work in one yard, Pavle moved to another backyard, and yet another. He was in the paradoxical position of being thankful that there was more wood to be split asunder, and of waiting for it to be finally over with.

After work he drove home slowly. He did not brush sawdust off his clothes. It stuck to his sweaty forehead. As he passed the house of a brother of his, he did not turn his head. His nephews and nieces stopped playing and stared at him in awe, whispering. Pavle had left the church, and for him who renounced Christ, it would be seven times more difficult to be saved than it would be for a nonbeliever.

Pavle, aware of his wife waiting for him, feared her bleak loneliness. Hearing the engine, she went into the kitchen and put several dry pieces of wood into the stove to warm the meal she had prepared by touch and smell.

Zora did have a social life—she chatted with her neighbors. Her sister-in-law walked her to and from the church, talking to her.

After sermons Zora held her chin up as if surveying a vast space. She puzzled over the voices, discerning vague family resemblances. She nodded her head and leaned it against her right palm. The sounds gave her clues of the past when she had dreamed of the future. Now she dreamed of the present, through the past, recognizing the voices she had known twenty years before and construing a picture the way someone gone to Australia daydreams about the people in the Old Country, across two oceans in either direction. Foreign friendliness murmured around her, clothes rustled, bones crackled in handshakes, lips smacked cheeks. *God-bless-you*s reached her ear, startling her whenever she realized they were for her.

Palms touched her right hand; the fingers embraced it like many small arms, gently. She shivered from the touch and loved the hands that reached out to her, out of the ghost world now made corporeal. Sometimes she knew the hands and not the voice, and sometimes she knew the voice, but not the hands, and sometimes she knew the hands and the voice, but not the lips that moistened her dry cheek. When the lips and the fingers parted from her, she stood in the pew, like a stone that the river passes.

Soon no one would address her anymore—the voices murmured, dissolving into the slow muddy-brown river. She had tried to imagine how the people looked, what colors they wore, and in her mind flowed only the old brown watercolors.

She created a world from a few sensory clues. The clues were torn, unnumbered pages of one ceaseless novel about a country that had exiled her without explanation. The wind tossed the pages away, so that she worried whether she could recapture the plot.

Every day after dinner, Pavle walked—slowly, moderately, as though he deemed reaching his destination not much preferable to being at any particular point in the walk. He was neither fat nor slim, and dressed neither poorly nor richly. This moderation gave him a gentlemanly air. If he had not had much success, well, he could repair that—each step well done and each precise unstrained gesture of his hands created an aura of dignity, not of enthusiasm or tragedy such as illusions spur. He seemingly walked neither in the path of Hedonism nor of Stoicism, but between pleasure and pain, unperturbed. His light brown hair, combed back, receded in the front, but he made no attempt to hide the recession.

In Pavle's nostalgic manner you could suspect that he savored forbearance, the way he drank wine that was neither too sweet nor too sour, yet sour enough to excite his Adam's apple to leap.

No matter how drunk he was, he did not swerve from his straight path. And the black glasses haunted him and asked, "And where now so late at night?"

One Sunday evening Pavle took a walk under orange clouds. His countenance bore a self-absorbed expression, though his self absorbed him least of all. He walked somewhat impatiently, as if wishing that the street blocks were shorter, over the bridge into the park's alleys of clipped tree crowns and fountain snakes squirting water through their eyes. He breathed in the cool air and smelled moist amber leaves. When he came out into the clearing for the rails, coal steam and smoke hovered and the rails clanked, though the train was out of sight.

He entered a beech grove, dark, though the tips of the trees glowed with the sun. He drank cold water from a spring and let it flow over his arms to cool his blood. He climbed a steep hill into the oak grove to a Jewish cemetery overgrown with bushes. Pavle took a brief rest, leaning against a tilting tombstone. The cool air moved noiselessly, making the flushed treetops quiver before they sank into darkness. When he reached the top of the hill, the sunshine had left even the high evergreens and withdrawn into the clouds. He walked onto a gravel path, where a dog began his fervent cold war against him from behind a wooden fence. The narrow space below the planks could accommodate only a closed muzzle. The dog had a dilemma: to bark without showing his teeth or to show his teeth and be quiet. He alternated, and occasionally found a hole through which to do both.

A car passed by and raised a cloud of brown dust. Pavle held his breath till the dust settled. The veins on his forehead protruded crookedly.

An insomniac rooster shrieked somewhere in the neighborhood, and his shrieks echoed from the vineyard hills on both sides of the road that split into a broad one flanked with houses and a narrow one entangled in vines. At the forking road stood a cross with a porcelain Jesus. The thorns of his crown were so large that he looked like a contrite, defrocked Statue of Liberty.

Pavle came to the small whitewashed house where his mistress Katitza lived. The door opened as if by itself, and no one came out. Soon after his entering, a lantern was lit. The town was suffering one of its usual blackouts, sinking into the previous century from which it had never quite emerged. Around the orange flicker of the lantern golden rays formed a halo.

Guitar sounds pulsed from the house, dispersed by the winds over the dark vineyards. Pavle's voice, deep and unsonorous, carried melancholy melodies from Croatian Zagorye, "Wine, wine … you are my porcupine; Rhein, Rhein, why can't you decline," and so on in that vein and in other veins to be filled with wine.

The following morning, instead of Pavle walking in the park in his leisurely Sunday manner, a voice went from mouth to mouth, through the ears of many. It traveled somehow as slowly as he had walked. Pavle had died making love to Katitza.

Dying in his orgasm—while Katitza had passed out from alcohol—he clasped her tightly in his embrace. By the time she woke up, he was dead, and cold, and well advanced in his rigor mortis. She could not get out of his grip. She screamed. At dawn, late drunks swerved by the house on the way home and listening to her got erections and admired her orgasmic passion and envied Pavle's skill and prowess.

At sunrise, when the screaming had not ceased, people who had gone to bed early, happy, sober and wise noticed there was something unearthly and unsettling in the shrieks. When they broke through the door, they saw a green woman with bulging eyes clasped by a yellow corpse. The icy corpse and its feverish prisoner were taken, naked, to the People's Hospital. Only when the doctors had cut his tendons could his embrace be unclasped.

When two male nurses brought Pavle on a stretcher into his home, they found Zora seated at the table, tirelessly waiting. She walked to the corpse and touched it with the tips of her fingers. His hands were wrapped in thick layers of cloth, like boxing gloves.

For all Zora knew, the night had killed Pavle. While her neighbors went out to buy a casket, she washed and oiled his body. Her neighbors helped her bend his arms backward, enough to slide him into his shirt, and then the arms sprang back and the hands met in unison as if for prayer. In the varnished fir casket, supine, he looked like a dead dignitary of the church contemplating the vastness of God's grace.

She placed four candles around him, one toward each corner of our square earth. It was so blazingly hot outside that the heat seeped in through the bricks. Zora's calico tomcat sniffed the corpse, crying like a sick baby. Waving his tail about, he knocked down a candle. The tablecloth caught fire and the flames licked the casket greedily and obscenely. Zora grabbed a pail of water from the chair and watered the fire. The flames went out and the wood resin hissed in steam. Zora blew out the remaining candles. The heat continued to radiate through the walls, entering the corpse, which swelled like a leavened loaf and pressed against the squeaking wood.

The mortician couldn't close the casket. To his suggestion that he pierce a hole in the corpse so the air and water could leak out, Zora declined, and the mortician then nailed laths of wood he found in Pavle's workshop atop the casket to increase its depth. He hammered on the lid; some nails peered through the wood outward, others inward, and only a few sank straight into the wood.

At the funeral, when the brass band took a break, half a dozen paces away from the hearse one could hear the crackling of casket wood. The corpse continued to bloat. A putrid smell spread through the cracks and permeated the steamy heat. Frightened by the stench and the creaking, the horses foamed at the mouth. The coachman barely restrained them from taking off at a gallop like dogs with tin cans tied to their tails.

In front of the hearse walked only women; behind, the relatives, and after them only men. Zora walked with her son and daughter holding her by her white-gloved arms; beneath her dark glasses tears flowed past her red nose.

At the grave pit, Pavle's relatives, dressed in black and white, solemnly stared at the casket from which came crackles and farts.

When the casket began to sink into the ground, Zora's lips muttered so fervently that it seemed they twitched; she prayed. The ropes rasped the wood and the casket dropped into the ground with a thud. Her son and daughter nudged her to drop the first fistful of soil into the pit, but she pushed them away and shrieked a high-pitched shriek, like a doe being slaughtered by wolves. The crowd gasped and blood scurried away from their faces. As if she had heard the goose-bumped crowd's blood rushing in sympathetic terror, she shouted shrilly back to them: "Up till now I prayed to God to bring him back to life. I believed He would. He won't! He won't! I can't believe any longer!"

For days and months after the funeral, Zora grieved with complete dedication as only a blind person could. She walked to his grave every day and put down tulips and carnations. The gravel in front of the grave cut into her knees. She caressed his silvery name on the varnished cross, dug with her fingers into the soil, and moved her ears as if she could hear his vehicle from blocks away, within the hollow ground. On rainy days she came to the grave just the same and listened to the frogs leap.

In the streets, Pavle's assistant limped, leaning on his bumpy cane. He stooped now more than when he had last worked with Pavle; his eyes were bluer, his face redder. When Zora walked past him, she swished her rod like a machete. The old peasant stood against the wall of his mildewed home, and the mortar sand behind his gaping boots trickled as though in an egg timer. Her broad nostrils sniffed the peasant's alcoholic aura. Saying nothing, she walked past him, but on one occasion, she said, "Why are you so quiet? Are you afraid of me?"

He invited her for tea laced with plum brandy and they talked about Pavle. He kept enumerating the good Pavle had done, how he had cut wood for various widows.

"That was not necessarily good," she said.

Whenever she walked by his home, he invited her in for tea. When he visited her, she baked loaves of bread for him. His rejuvenated look gave rise to the rumor that he had become Zora's lover.

She continued going to the church, where she waited for the sermon on Lazarus. She whispered prayers for Pavle. Nobody dared to tell her that Pavle perhaps didn't deserve so many prayers and so much grief.

One Christmas eve, she remained in the pews after the service. With her cane she walked to the Christmas tree, sniffed its green needles and touched its iron base where the mutilated trunk rested on the wooden floor. The veins of her fingers felt the missing roots and stuck to the resin that oozed as a heavy and frozen mixture of blood and sweat. She lit a match and dropped it. A flame burst out. The tree crackled and roared, its lingual shapes multiplied in size. She took off her glasses and smiled. The flames climbed the curtains, rushed down the carpeted aisle and entered the beams.

The church was a huge flame by dawn, a tongue of the earth licking the heavens. The flame spread to the neighboring bus garage, and the oily iron and tires joined the flame.

In the rubble of the collapsed church her skeleton coiled in the corner; she had died like blinded Samson among the Philistines, who had brought down the pillars with thousands of the enemy. After her death, the old peasant continued to limp in front of her house, his hair completely white, his blue irises ringed with the haze of cataracts. Leaning against his bumpy stick, now and then he lifted the brown hat off his head even though no one was passing by.

A DROP OF COGNAC

A decade ago, visiting my widowed cousin-in-law Ishtvan in Nizograd, Croatia, I was determined not to drink much; only perhaps two drinks, the optimum amount for the heart and mood. We placed on the table a bottle of cognac and a pack of cigarettes. We used to be Baptists, and this way of conversing, doing what we had been taught was wrong, gave an edge to our conversation perhaps unfamiliar to those who were not brought up in repressive churches.

"Just look around," said Ishtvan. "See how large and comfortable my house is? Did I build it? No, I only put the finishing touches to it. My father laid the foundation, raised it, put a roof over it; he built it by his own strength. We forget how much our fathers accomplished. We are proud, we have better opportunities, we are better educated; but look: what have we done?"

I replied, nothing, quietly resenting that he should place me in his category, though I was more than a decade younger than he. So, he expects I will accomplish nothing, I thought, and feared he might be right.

"Each of us carries his father in him," Ishtvan went on. "Mine I feel right here more and more," he pointed to his chest. "Now I am as old as he was when I was two years old. I am very similar to him; I feel that he is in my blood, in my motion; wherever I move, there is my father moving. When I have an intuition, it's my father speaking; sometimes it's unsettling. I am never free."

"How about your mother?"

"Well, her too. Even my grandmother. I am a walking cemetery of my family! Hahahaha!" He took another sip of cognac; the label read *aut Caesar aut nihil.* We knocked our pitifully small glasses, so small that you could rationalize to yourself that it was no more than a couple of drops you were drinking. Some of the brandy flew up and sprinkled us, like sacramental water.

"To your health!" we both said.

"I'll never forget the things my father taught me," he said, "things I have to remember over and over again. You see, some people are too proud, think too much of themselves. For example, your older brother. Granted, he is a doctor, but that does not mean that he could not return visits and phone calls. I have called him so many times, and guess how many times he has called me?"

I didn't like being put on the spot, as if I should be responsible for my brother. The number must be beyond, or rather below, any expectation; he would gladly see me incredulous. If I said "zero," I would take away some of his rhetorical pleasure. So, insincerely, I guessed, "Once a year."

"Well, my Yozzo! Not a sin-gle time! Anyway, let me tell you what my father taught me about pride. He took me into a wheat field and said, 'Now, son, choose the stalk of wheat with the most grains on it.' I looked around and plucked the tallest I could see. My father smiled, said 'Look, son,' and separated a multitude of tall stalks and among them found one, low, bent, and plucked that one. 'Let us count the grains!' His stalk carried at least twice as many grains as mine. 'See,' he said, 'the ones you cannot see because of the tall ones are the most laden ones. They are the best. Remember that! If you look for the best, don't look among those in the first rows, the proud ones.'

"I recalled his telling me the wheat parable only a week ago. Oh, I don't mean to say anything against your brother, I don't know why I brought him up, I must be getting drunk. Well, to your health!

"Our fathers outstripped us in everything, and we think that we are more unique. They thought more deeply than we do, and what I think now, he had already thought out for me.

"Yes, I am a walking cemetery of my family, and you know, I feel your cousin, Tanya, too, in my blood. Oh how she suffered! You know lupus erythematosus?"

"Yes, I guess so, the degenerative disease of the red blood cells."

"One organ after another is reduced to its minimal functioning, decomposes, and there is hardly anything of you left; you wonder how you can still be alive, a tingling body of pain. Tanya held through it all heroically.

"And you know what the 'Reverend' Iliya Lukich told me?" Ishtvan went to the cupboard, brought out two regular milk glasses, poured some cognac into them, and sucked out nearly the whole contents of his glass in a big gulp. "He used to tell me, you know, before she was taken ill, that I should mend my ways, return to the fold, repent, lest I should be visited upon with the iniquity of my deeds—that's how he used to express himself. He claimed he had visions about me; God told him a disaster would befall me, unless … You know how he was, always some visions and bullying."

"Yes, I know, once I broke my left arm, and in the youth group he said that God was warning the whole group against the sin of self-gratification! I told him that I was right-handed, so the warning was misplaced."

"Well, when he learned about Tanya's illness, he came to me fuming with triumph, and said, 'See, what did I tell you! It has come true. You haven't repented, and God is punishing you through her! She will die, and you will have to live with it! She will die because of YOU!'

"You know, her disease horrified me. The house looked doomed. When things are so bleak, you are liable to believe almost anything. Your mind cannot work then. It had better not work! How else can you face reality? I tried to repudiate what Iliya said—oh, he's just a joker, things just happen, that's all there is to it. But in vain did I try. Each day as she withered away, and you know that she had been beautiful, my heart shrank. The more she withered, the more wretched I was. I drank savagely then, and fought in the bars, just to relieve myself. Oh, not to relieve myself, quite the contrary, to degrade myself, it's true, I am the sinner, it's all because of me!

"It was worse when I was sober. I could not harm myself. I was winning all my fights, against all odds, and people are scared of me."

"Yes, I heard that you beat three policemen, piled them on top of each other outside the Happy Cellar. Did you really do it?"

"Oh, yes!" His voice, low and slow and falling apart under the burden of memories, now became resonant. "I used to box seriously. For a year I was a pro in Argentina. I had the skill and the strength. And since then you should see how they respect me, the cops!"

He grew silent and it was already becoming dark outside. As we did not turn on the lights, I could no longer see his features, and his face was merely a heavy silhouette. The sky was dark blue, and it was bound to grow darker.

"You know, one of the worst things about growing older is that your strength leaves you. As your powers diminish, so does your self-reliance. I used to think when I was your age that I could do anything. Now I doubt everything."

His voice became low and slow. "What anguish that was when she was dying! She was in this room. I took out the bed after her death and burned it. I wonder why I continue to live in this house. I guess I like the memory of her. And where could I go anyway?"

I could not reply to that.

"Every day when I came home from work I saw her here, right where you are sitting, or in the white hospital. Her hair fell out, her eyebrows did, too, she was pale yellow. Her eyes were red, without luster, her face contorted, there was something saintly in her face; sometimes a glow would return and she would whisper to me how happy she was that she would see God, how she loved me, how to have courage. I am happy she had so much faith! I had none.

"Then she would have another relapse, her eyes would be swollen, and her face shriveled up, her body too, she could not even whisper. I watched her for hours and shivered with horror and disgust. Yet, I could not move my eyes away from her. I longed for the dark to come, just as it is coming now, and when it did, I wished to turn on the lights. But then I was afraid of what I would see of her. How much dread I experienced! I never thought it possible. And that is all because of your sins! I continued repeating to myself. All because of your blasphemies, debauchery. I am a murderer."

"But," I said and my voice was feeble because of not having said anything for a while—I cleared my throat—"Why should she suffer for what you did? You know, if I killed someone, my brothers would not have to answer for that in the court, just me alone. Don't you think God's justice would be the same, provided He existed? If you sinned, you'd suffer for it, not she."

Here he took a deep smoke, and so did I. In the dark I saw only the small red circle of his cigarette as he inhaled, and then it receded into a dull ash-filtered glow.

"Well, we rarely suffer for what we have done, it is usually for what others have done, and they rarely suffer for what they have done, but for what we have done! That's the whole idea of

Christianity! You don't get punished for your own sin; somebody else does. She was a Christ for me ... but there is no salvation here.

"When Iliya told me she suffered because of me, I believed it. You have no idea what savagery conscience is capable of! If I could be in hell then, I thought, it would console me! The squirming of my flesh in the fire would set things right; being tortured to the utmost and still kept alive so I could be tortured more, forever and ever. I would be relieved! What a wonderful place hell must be. But the most painful thing about hell is that it does not exist! That's what tortured me—that I could not be tortured, that I walked about brimming with health and strength, smelling the southern flowery winds in the spring and listening to swallows return from the Mediterranean!

"I still cannot understand where the illness came from. It's a rare disease."

"Maybe a genetic accident," I said. "An inner Chernobyl."

"Accident?" He looked at me quizzically and ironically.

"Anyway," he went on, "you know how Iliya went around, preaching against sins, laying his hands on the sick, bragging how God cured the people through him. And lo and behold, you know what happened?"

"His wife got sick."

"Yes, almost as soon as Tanya had died, Iliya's wife, Vera, contracted the same disease, lupus! And with her the progress of the disease was in the beginning as rapid as with Tanya, but before she would die, she hovered in that agony for four years! Iliya prayed over her; he constantly laid his hands on her, he had visions of her being healed, he prayed his prayers in all the churches around, but nothing. She died a month ago. She died a much longer and worse death than Tanya.

"Half a year ago I went to him, to return his visit, and said to him, "You boastful saint, remember what you told me when Tanya was ill, that she was dying because of my sins? And now, what do you say now, for whose sins is your wife dying?"

There was a glee of victory gleaming out of my ex-cousin-in-law. "Ha, what do you say? Almost enough to return to the faith of our fathers!"

He turned on the light. Blinking, I tried to pour a shot of cognac, but only one amber drop slid out.

PINTARIC THE TOWN PHILOSOPHER

My friends and I loved misfits and odd characters as they entertained us. Not much happened in Daruvar, an old hot-springs spa (Aqua Belissae, Muddy Water, in the Roman Empire), where time seems to have stood for centuries, and we were eager for events.

In the 1970s, Gospodin Pintaric frequently stood in the center of Daruvar with his ornate walking stick, which he used for a variety of purposes—to ward off stray dogs, to wave in the air when making a particularly emphatic point, like a symphony conductor, pointing it toward the sky, and to knock on the hollow chestnut tree near a newsstand with such force that sometimes chestnuts clattered down on us, and we, a few gymnasium students, listened to him as though he were Plato. He compared his walking stick to the staff of Moses—only there was no Red Sea to separate here.

As a Rosicrucian, he elucidated to us numerology and various other esoteric sciences. He encouraged us to grow our hair long as antennae, to receive messages from the universe via iron, copper, and other metals in our hair. He tied his hair in a pony-tail, and his face emitted several shaky strands of gray hair gathered in a point, which failed to hide his receded chin. He had worked in Germany and returned home before he could collect his pension plan, and sued the West German government to gain disability payments.

Although he lived in the winemaking hills, he despised the alcoholic culture. He described the Yugoslav tri-color flag as Wine, Rakija, Beer, and the Marxist lifestyle as u-se na-se i poda-se (into onto and under yourself). I gave up on listening to him, as I was not interested in the variety of esoteric sciences coming from all sorts of unreliable sources. I wanted to read the philosophers for myself. At the time, I had my own brand of religious mysticism, and I tended to torment my friends with long discourses about the spiritual composition of matter. Moreover, his habit of touching our antennae, to make points, and sometimes of raising his walking stick above our heads if we didn't agree with him, didn't agree with me.

In a small town like ours, a solitary man who gathered boys drew some suspicion. A somewhat older friend of mine asked, What do you think, what does Pintaric like more, Plato's idealism or Plato's boys? I have no idea, I answered—he does like ideas. He influenced a few kids in our town to read religious texts, philosophy, parapsychology, and so on. A man like Pintaric would hardly be possible now in the streets of a small town, which was the size that Plato thought was the maximum and optimal size for a functional democracy, 8,000 people. Anyhow, a small town with a peripatetic culture was great for discussions. We didn't watch much television; cinema had a poor program; and many of us high-schoolers spent evenings discussing politics, religion, and so on, when we didn't talk about soccer and rock. The older people were mostly conservative and didn't make good conversationalists for Pintaric, unlike the peripatetic youngsters.

There were anecdotes about him: When Pintaric returned from Germany, his neighbor was taken ill, and Pintaric drove her to the emergency room in his blue Mercedes. The next day, to thank him, she invited him to dinner at home for one meal, and he joined her and the family. He understood it not just as one dinner but as a nightly occasion for years to come, and the family didn't mind him for a few weeks. But when he began to teach them to keep the fork on the left of the plate and how to tuck cloth napkins, the hostess objected that if he didn't like their style, he'd better leave. He felt offended and slapped her hard across the cheek so that she fell. She was not of the weak variety, however, weighing some 100 kilograms, about 220 pounds. She got up and grabbed his walking stick and beat him with it, so that he had to go to the ER, full of bruises, wilts, and all sorts of aches. His disability-claim process was not settled yet so he sold his Mercedes and lived poorly, on social aid, which consisted of one free lunch in the central tavern, Kapelica (Little Chapel). Every day he walked down the hill to the central kiosk, where he picked up the daily newspaper, Vecernji List, and read it quickly, start to finish, and returned it without paying for it.

Using the kiosk side windows as mirrors, he'd comb his long hair and scraggly beard with an enormous comb. After lunch, he contributed to the well-being of the town. He descended into Daruvarsku podrum (Daruvar Cellar) where he sought chronic alcoholics. He walked with them to his home and performed his special exorcism rituals around a fire that he made in the middle of his one-room house. Days later, if he saw the men whom he had thus cured drinking again at the Cellar, he would bang with his stick on the oiled beechwood floor, and in a voice two octaves lower than his usual voice, he said, "But you have promised never to drink again!" So some alcoholics feared him, but the bartender, who didn't want to see his business dwindle any further as it verged on bankruptcy, forbade Pintaric from visiting and chasing away regular customers without whom no bar can succeed.

Eventually, when nobody believed in his power of visualization (for years he said he visualized a letter in German, granting him the disability status), he got a letter from Germany informing him that soon he would get ten years back pay and then regular payments, a handsome sum, in Deutschmarks. It is not clear how he celebrated, but the news was too much for him. He died two days later, and because nobody wanted to suffer his exorcism rituals upon visiting him at home, it took two weeks before his body was discovered sprawled on the floor, way past rigor mortis. Since it was winter, a severe one, he hadn't rotted, though some people claim that rats had chewed on his carcass. That may be an embellishment of a mean town's imagination. I haven't seen his corpse, nor did I attend his small funeral, but have heard that in death he looked as tranquil as he did after finishing his speeches, sitting down under a chestnut tree on a bench, spiritually fulfilled.

If I thought Pintaric had nothing to do with me, I was wrong. My older brother, Vlado, an ophthalmologist, told me we were related to Pintar. Our grandmother Juza from Prague and Pintaric's father were cousins. How many degrees of separation is that, I asked my brother? Six? According to a theory, we are all six degrees separated at most, and Vlado replied, Yes, that applies to who knows whom, but this is blood relation.

Now that years have passed, and I think of where I will age and retire, it occurs to me that if I were to return to Daruvar, where many of my friends already have died and others are gone without plans to return, that maybe I would become a Pintaric, walking around town with a stick, talking nebulously to whoever would listen.

With a glass of red wine in my hand, or not. Who's to know?

DRY LAW

Now and then I plug the jug, as the expression goes. In 2006, I went to Russia with my family. I decided that I would not drink while in Russia as drinking there is famously perilous. We arrived in minus twenty degrees Celsius weather, and it was still dark at ten in the morning. I found a Kofye Hauz, a block away from where we rented the apartment in St. Petersburg. Every dawn, at nine a.m., I went to the café and drank cappuccinos, and the waitresses, as soon as they saw me, would say, Dvoynoi cappuccino? Da, double, pozhalusta! I didn't miss alcohol at all, with such good coffee, although the coffee shop offered absinthe and whiskey. I was supposed to be a Fulbright research fellow and to give a few lectures at the St. Petersburg State University, but nobody ever got in touch with me to offer me an office or to ask me to lecture, which was just fine with me. I only visited the university to have my visa extended, which a man did, without saying a word. The coffee shop would be my office, and I'd write there, but my family and I were a bit socially isolated, and so we organized a literary party. Russian poets, such as Arkady Dragomoschenko and Sasha Skidan read; my friend David Stromberg read an excerpt from his novel about an alcoholic Russian immigrant in Jerusalem; and many people I didn't know read, such as the tall and thin poet, Pavel. I got them all plenty of wine but I didn't drink any of it. Pavel did, and he vomited all over the apartment. Jeanette was scandalized—you call those people poets? They are just drunks. Don't invite them again. I am glad that at least you don't drink.

I was glad too. Forty days went by, and we decided to go to Moscow to visit my childhood friend Bozo, the Croatian ambassador. In Moscow both my daughter and wife had food poisoning from the food on the train. Moreover, for some reason, we had a hard time finding the embassy and the street, so we wandered in deep snow and the wind. Exhausted and frozen, we were relieved to see my friend in warm spaces, and to drink Russian tea. How about some vodka? offered Bozo. No, I don't drink at all. That's impressive, he said. The second day, Bozo said, How about some Vranac from Montenegro? It's really good. Don't tempt him, his wife said, Didn't he tell you loud and clear that he is a non-alcoholic? Yes, he did, Bozo said. I intervened, Well, the wine makes me nostalgic, I'll have just a little glass, and I'll pretend it didn't happen. I will stay on the wagon. Great idea, said Bozo. He poured me a glass—we clinked and drank. It was good indeed. We ended up drinking, among the four adults, two bottles, and our mood was excellent. We repeated the exercise the following evening.

Back in St. Petersburg, I didn't drink for two days, but then, we had visitors, Boris and Natasha, a violinist and his wife, a painter, who gave my daughters art lessons. To host them, I got some red wine and cooked salmon ... I drank too.

As if to spite me, a wine shop opened across from us on Griboyedova. I bought a bunch of Spanish and Georgian wines. Now with meals we had wine: I definitely was not on the wagon, but deceived myself by declaring that I was on the moderation wagon with no more than three glasses a day. I became a regular customer at the wine shop, and sometimes the wine was exceedingly bitter because clearly, it had nearly frozen in transport, but that didn't prevent me from this form of evening relaxation.

If a politician got me off the wagon, a bigger politician intervened and threatened to help. Putin came to my aid. Namely, he outlawed all Georgian products, including the mineral water Borjomi, and especially Georgian wines. For a while, all the alcoholic products were outlawed in Russia, and a strange disquiet wafted through the streets of St. Petersburg. People walked more quickly and aggressively than before. The newspapers gave an explanation: The government had to do a precise inventory of the stock in the country. Much of the wine was not regulated enough, so now it would be monitored better and it would be safer. By some estimates, about 30,000 people had died that year from ingesting samogon (home distilled moonshine) and other alcoholic products containing methyl alcohol. So, it was like another Sukhoi Zakon. Dry law. Gorbachev introduced it a while back and that precipitated his demise. For several days I had nothing to drink, and I was beginning to feel fresher, and thought, the hell with it, it's for the best. But on one occasion, in a twenty-four-chasa store, I noticed a few bottles of red wine, which the attendant sold me at twice the previous price. And so, not even Putin could help me.

ON QUITTING ALCOHOL

La Distillerie is the name of the Montreal bar where I am writing this essay. I needed to leave my apartment but didn't know where to go at eleven in the evening, other than to the corner bar three blocks away. You can't just stay indoors all day or you'll go insane, or from lack of motion get sick with diabetes or something. And I don't know any other magnet toward which to gravitate late at night other than a bar. I am drinking Pellegrino here, with ice, while people are drinking gins and tonics, cognacs, and other perilous substances. And the subject I want to write on is abstinence. You know, from booze. Anyway, you can quit religion, but you can still orient yourself by the beauties of various churches and cathedrals and temples and mosques in a city. Cities would look terrible, would lose their souls, without steeples and domes, and likewise, without cafés and bars. I don't want to drink, but I still like the dark atmosphere with rock music. Anyway, I am done with booze but not with public establishments. Here, I can concentrate on my banal subject matter, banal and necessary.

It's easy to quit booze; I've done it many times. I am paraphrasing Mark Twain who joked about quitting nicotine. Unlike with booze, I've had good luck quitting nicotine—I was addicted to smoking when I was twelve; I stole packs of cigarettes from tourists, from Alfa Romeos of Italians who came to hunt wild boar in my hometown. But at the Adriatic, after discovering a nude beach where I went swimming and became a pretty good diver with improved lung capacity—I swam under Western capitalist women and looked up to see sunshine refracting and hairs like seaweed swaying gently (capitalist women didn't shave four decades ago)—I completely lost the smoking habit and became athletic. Lost interest in cigarettes, other than for a month ten years later when I house-sat for a wealthy manufacturer and tried to write on typewriters. Upon getting bronchitis, I said, the hell with this, and never looked at cigarettes with desire again. I hardly drank until the age of twenty. In Novi Sad at the end of the first year of medical school, I had a few shots of plum brandy with my roommates, and one of them commented, Who knew you could be fun. Your jokes are really good. You were so damned serious all year long. I was surprised at my euphoric state—it was a combination of acing human anatomy, most dreaded subject, as well as plum brandy. When I announced to my friends that I was quitting medicine to study psychology in the States, they said, OK, now you are no longer funny but insane.

In the States, at Vassar, everybody tended to go to Matthew's Mug, local pub, to drink beer and vodka tonics and dance to disco, but I preferred to drink coffee and eat bagels with my philosophical friends, disdaining drinking. My roommate, however, who was a fireman and economics major, nearly thirty-years-old, had a collection of whiskey and cognac, and he attended wine tasting classes and told me that in order to become rich he needed to be able to socialize with the rich, which meant drinking single malts and fine reds. Every night, he'd offer me a shot of whiskey, and the first semester I always said no, but the second semester, during a deep winter, I occasionally said yes. His method seemed to work; he married a heiress.

The drinking age then was eighteen, and I couldn't understand all the frolicking and vomiting, etc. While I was transferring credits from the medical school, the assistant dean in charge of transfer students, a graceful Dutch lady, was puzzled as to why I wanted to finish college in two years when I had it so good, and she said, OK, do describe to me your education. We'll have a picnic, I do want to understand why you quit medicine and came here. And she picked me up in a red Porsche and asked whether I wanted to drive, and I said I didn't know how to. When she offered me some French Bordeaux-supérieur, I said I didn't really drink. She laughed and said, So you read Hegel, and you can't drive and don't know what to do with fine red wine, and you've never had Brie? You are a noble savage! She proceeded to teach me how to drive stick shift and then gave me a glass of wine, which I gulped with clicks in my throat like it was cranberry juice. No, sip it, go slowly, this is not a sports car, it's wine. And actually don't drink right away, let it breathe first, let it get used to air, to you, and then kiss it and savor it. Anyway, this lady converted me to enjoying wines. I did explain to the Dean the structure of Yugoslav gymnasium, which I deemed the equivalent of one year of college, and the credits from one year of med school, at least one more. She researched through the Institute of International Education and said, Guess what, you are completely right. And so, after a few bottles of superb French wines, I was advanced from freshman to junior, concluding that there was much educational power in Margaux.

And a decade later, when my cholesterol was high, I bought into the whole health wine propaganda. I needed to keep my arteries clear, not to die, like my father, who had been a teetotaller all his life. *Živili, Na zdravlje, Santé, Zum Wohl,* etc. But the pros and cons for drinking clearly make alcohol a losing game. Pros: occasional good moods, some cardiac benefits in moderate drinking. Cons: liver damage, brain damage, cancer risks, cumulative expenses, accident proneness, potential for social embarrassment, for saying inappropriate things, for showing up at work late, and basically for making one's family and oneself miserable, if not injured, and a huge waste of time—while drinking, you can't work, and if you drink too much, you need a few hours in the morning to begin functioning properly. Oh, and the heart benefits—at more than three drinks, when you lose muscle coordination, so does your heart, and you actually damage and enlarge the heart muscle, and increase blood pressure. Maybe it's like aspirin, if you have a mini dose every day, your heart benefits, but try to have five aspirin tablets a day, and you shall bleed to death. So no wonder many people decide to quit booze if they can't moderate it.

And what is moderation? Once, I declared to my friend, editor of Fiction Magazine, Moshe Mirsky, that I had quit drinking. He turned to me, and in his startled dramatic fashion, with his curly white hair leaping all around his head, said, Quit? My friend, the Talmud exhorts that one should drink wine moderately. Drinking two bottles a day would be immoderation, and drinking nothing at all, is also extreme and immoderate. I warn you, don't do it.

Here are a couple of examples of the lives of my friends who decided to quit. Calvin, a big black dude, the former bass player with Soul Machine, a band in Arizona. He was my roommate in Las Vegas for half a year when I wrote a terrible novel about Russia. I asked him to celebrate with me when I thought the writing was going well, to share a bottle of Grgich Zinfandel. He said, I haven't had a drink in twenty-seven years. Why is that? After we had a big concert in Phoenix, the day after it, when we seemed to be getting big, I woke up in my Ford Mustang in mid-air. I'd had a bottle of Jack Daniels and many lines of cocaine. My car flew into someone's yard, hit the wall, and became an accordion. Somehow, I crawled out unscathed. That I was so dazed seemed normal, so the cops didn't test my alcohol levels, which must have been astronomical. I got a written warning, Failure to Control Vehicle. In the meanwhile, perhaps in those few minutes, the only sober man from our band, the drummer, was killed in a car crash. Robbers running away from cops after stealing money from a convenience store ran the red light and smashed into his car, and he was dead. So, there I was, I should have died, and he died instead, like Christ, for my sins. That's how I saw it. You could have seen it differently. Being sober in that case may have proved dangerous, and your drinking saved you. No, my friend, that's not how it is. I've been much happier since. I recommend it, would you like to go to AA meetings with me?

I had another friend and roommate three decades ago, Ed, a news photographer for *The New York Times*, who quit. His story: he was in love with a woman but too shy to talk to her. One New Year's Eve party he finally had a chance to meet her. He drank a lot to encourage himself to approach her and passed out, and in the morning he complained to his friends that he fucked up. I could have talked to her. Talked to her? his friends said. That you sure did, and not only that, you two had sex in front of everybody on the bed over all the guests' coats and jackets, a Kama Sutra demonstration. And so Ed said, If this was supposed to be the best moment of my life and I don't remember it even happening because of alcohol, I am quitting. And he did. He chewed tobacco, smoked, had many bad habits, but not booze anymore.

I had a couple of wake-up calls. Once, I was drunk with my publisher from Story Press in Cincinnati. We left Kaldi's bar in the black ghetto downtown, a heavily policed area, where the cops had incited race riots after killing sixteen young Black men in a row in drug wars. As soon as I made a U-turn, where it was illegal, two cop cars flashed at me, and the cops came out and said, Sir, have you been drinking. I said, No. They said, We saw you stagger out of a bar. We are gonna test you. I was terrified—that would mean license suspension, a ticket of at least a thousand USD. As I stepped out, their walkie-talkies went off. A quick conversation ensued, and one cop said, You are lucky we have a homicide to attend to. Someone else isn't lucky. Goodbye, and don't drink and drive, buddy! Actually, I may have been within legal limits, as you can metabolize one beer an hour, and you can have the alcohol content of two in your bloodstream and be marginal. Still, if I had gotten a DUI, I could, for example, never have immigrated to Canada, to Quebec, to be specific, which seems strange because a big part of Montreal's economy is alcoholic tourism, all the underage kids from the United States coming up here to pass out.

I quit drinking once for forty days, until I got the news that a friend of mine shot himself. He was a Jewish English radiologist who was earning fifty thousand dollars a month, married to a French snob. She drove him crazy and left him, and instead of celebrating, the guy shot himself. I happened to have a bottle of unopened wine, which for forty days I had no interest in, but now, I thought, I have to drink in my friend's honor. Well, I drank the following day, too, and that quitting episode failed.

On another occasion, I quit drinking for six months after falling off a tall deck in Ohio. I went out to admire the stars while taking a leak and didn't see the edge of the deck, went over it, and fell on a rock, cracking half the rack of ribs on my right side. The excruciating pain taught me good lessons. Don't drink and look at the sky at the same time. Or just don't drink, and do look at the sky. And don't take painkillers. I have no idea what's so good about them. I found them to dehydrate me, stupify and dizzify me, and basically, I don't need much help to become stupid. I found them annoying and preferred sheer pain.

In my sixth month of not drinking, I made friends with Robert at the soon-to-be-suicidal Englishman's party. Robert, also an Englishman, a lawyer specializing in international liquor law, imported wines and gave me a case of the best Fess Parker for my book party in Pittsburgh. Everybody drank, and I thought, Well, I will have a couple of glasses, too, but only today. I had more than a couple, and when I stepped into the dark, I stepped over an uneven stone and sprained my ankle. That didn't teach me to hop right back on the wagon. Instead, I kept getting together with

Robert for wine tastings. He talked poetically about wines, and I tested him once, and he couldn't tell the difference between his Merlots and Cabs, despite the poetry or perhaps because of it. His favorite was 100 Bitches, 100 Roaches, as it came from the highest altitudes in France, from one of the oldest vineyards, so the roots sucked lots of minerals, and you could, of course, taste the minerals. Yes, that's why we drank, to taste the zinc. Pretty much the same reason people eat raw oysters, no?

Last year again I quit for a hundred days and felt great. Then I arrived in Tbilisi, and a friend of mine there told me she had cancer and only a few months to live. We were having a welcome party, a feast, with fancy Georgian wines in earthenware, and after hearing her story, I thought, What the hell, this is too much. I'll have a couple of glasses to sympathize. The following day we had a tour of some of the oldest wineries in the world, so while listening to the history of wine, of how the word *gvino*, in Georgian, *wine*, is the origin of the word wine, how Georgian wine was seven thousand years old (now it's 7,001), older than the Biblical world, which is supposed to be not even six thousand-years-old, and when invited to taste wine fermented as it was in the beginning, under the ground in huge jugs, of course, I tasted some, and pretty soon it was clear that I was not on the wagon anymore.

Well, it's easy to quit. You know, De Quincy bragged about quitting in *Confessions of an English Opium-Eater*. Yes, while writing the book, he abstained, but after he published it, he got enough money to keep up the old habit. Sure, it takes money to keep going. And I have done it again. I have quit. I feel like a champ. And now I am not going to digest tragedies with a glass of wine, nor celebrate good events with a glass of wine. I might even attend an AA meeting to see whether that gives me firmer and steadier resolve to be on the wagon. (I actually want to attend an AA meeting because I want to write a silly story about AA). Next time something bad happens, I will think, It could be worse if I get drunk. And if something good happens, I'll say, It's great, why ruin it with risky poisons? If one wants to drink, there's always a reason to drink. And if one enjoys life, or suffers, there's always a good reason not to drink. Things could always become worse. I'd rather be drunk than old; lyrics of an old Serbian folk song, translated: It's worse to be both drunk and old. At least I can be sober and conscious. OK, I won't exaggerate about consciousness.

Will I never drink again? That seems like a sad proposition. Really, life has to be a moody affair, without reprieve? Hm, but yes, I can look at the sky. "While I kiss the sky," said Jimi Hendrix ... well, not exactly an example of sobriety. But being sober for days, alert and calm, with my blood pressure falling from high to the low normal range, that feels like a great state of intoxication. I've never had heroin, but perhaps that's what heroin addicts aim for, this kind of calm and peace. It turns out that the best mind-expanding drug is water with a lemon twist. The hell with it, I'll have another Pellegrino, and I don't envy the seemingly euphoric drunks around me.

That reminds me of how some thirty-five-years-ago, my friend Boris and I got together with an acquaintance of mine, a Hungarian Baptist twenty-two-year-old nurse, a striking tall and graceful woman, and we invited her to a Biergarten in downtown Stuttgart. My sister, a cardiac nurse in Stuttgart, had introduced us. Boris and I had beer, which displeased Martha, and while sipping her mineral water, she looked around at the drunken people who sang and toasted and laughed, and said, Just look at them. They think they are happy, and they are not aware at all how profoundly unhappy they are. Boris and I ordered another round. Wow, I said, I didn't know fresh Warsteiner tasted so much better than bottled. This is amazing! Boris, are we profoundly unhappy? I asked. Profoundly, he answered. I never saw her again, but I saw many a beer mug afterwards.

That reminds me—don't mind me, many things remind me—of my asking a cab driver in Dublin where the best tavern for fresh Guinness was. He said, Wrong man to ask, I don't drink. Really, but you are Irish. Yes, they haven't revoked my citizenship, strangely enough, he said. How is that possible? Like this: I was drinking too much, and I was engaged to a young lady, and she said, Listen Fred, it's either me or booze. Oh, dear, I said. I won't drink again, and you know what, I never did and don't miss it at all. Your wife must be proud of you. Oh, I quit her, too, a week later. She didn't realize what she was proposing. I liked her when drunk, but without booze, she seemed too bossy.

Anyway, now at La Distillerie, I wonder, Was Martha wrong? I look around, people laugh too loudly for my taste—humor I enjoy, but let's not have loud spasms over it—and think, Are they happy? Well, you know, who knows. To my health, I tell myself, because who will talk to a sober man in a bar anyway, *Na zdravlye*, and I drink the best blood-thinner and tranquilizer in the world, water.

CODA:

RASPUTIN IS LIT

In Grisha's hungover state, the low sunshine of the mid-May morning glared and hurt his eyes. He cleared his throat and spat. His esophagus still burned as though on fire, and when he exhaled, smoke or steam came out of him. The night before, he had visited an old-style vodka tavern such as still existed only in Siberia (a wooden hut serving nothing but vodka) at the crossroads near Pokrovskoye, his village. He had spent all his money, and in the end gave up his sheepskin jacket, and his shirt, and his bronze necklace with a cross, and he would have given up his pants, too, but the barman laughed and said, You'd have to pay someone to wear that! How did you manage to rip a hole like that? Your farts are that powerful?

No, I sat on a rock. And how about the boots? asked Grisha. They are made out of ox hide.

They look terrible and useless, too. They don't even seem to have soles—you dropped them somewhere?

I'll give you everything for one more glass of vodka, and you can give me your sackcloth so I wouldn't go home naked.

Sackcloth? What do you think, what era do you live in? Even an empty potato sack would be worth more than what you have. This is the end of your drinking for the night. One more glass and you'd have to crawl home.

Grisha had woken up in a ditch right outside of his two-story home. He had no recollection how he'd got there, whether he had walked or whether someone had dumped him. A red-eyed, perhaps blind goose had awoken him, mistaking his hair for grass and pecking at it. As he sat up, she hissed at him and he tried to kick her.

Grisha covered his eyes with his palms, massaged them, and looked after the flying goose. The sun flared up through tiny leaves of oaks, green, and brilliant. The boughs spread out like huge arms; welcoming arms, looming in the light. They were thick black arms, with refracting light thinning them.

He passed by a large possession of a peasant. Geese were honking at him and sticking out their necks. There were tall haystacks, protected with wooden fences from deer and thieves. The wood wasn't just branches but narrow and hewn round laths. With these laths, one should make something much nicer. If he collected enough of them, he could make a sweat lodge.

He went home, hitched his old, emaciated black horse to a squealing cart, and collected a sharpened axe and a rusty saw. He rode back to the peasant's field, chopped and sawed the laths into the right size, and loaded them on the dusty cart.

The grass was turning green but was not tall yet. The soil was wet, and his boots got muddied. As he walked, they were sucked into the mud, and when he pulled them out, the mud sucked loudly after them, asking to swallow them again. The mud tried to eat his boots, displaying its bad manners, smacking its lips and slurping, but the boots pulled out, up, and then hovered before hitting the salivating mouth of toothless Mother Earth. The soil succeeded in taking off his left boot. Grisha stood like a stork, a gangly and yet sturdy stork, on one leg. The wet cloth wrapped around his foot unraveled and fell into the mud, revealing his large feet; his uncut nails curved and wrapped his large toes, thus giving them extra protection. Grisha swore, Fuck St. Catherine! He pulled out the boot, which was now filled with water, and emptied the water from it, and then slid his foot back in, as he continued to haul the beautiful wood from the fence to his cart.

The horse waited patiently on the road, dropping steamy dung now and then for entertainment. Grisha carried the wood. One plank gave him a splinter, and his hand bled.

Suddenly, the peasant came out from his house, running. He was clad all in brown and his face was brown, too, weathered and creased. He had a long, broad nose with a horizontal crack in the middle. It seemed a sword must have hit him across the nose, cutting a wedge into it.

Grisha was tempted to run, but he looked into the peasant's eyes—they were pale blue like his. He seemed to be very similar to Grisha—perhaps a remote uncle? Maybe even his father?

You dirty ass, you're destroying my fences. You'll have to pay!

I am doing nothing of the sort. I will use the wood for better purposes. It's a sin to let such beautiful wood rot in the fields, and to keep God's creatures away from the grass.

I'll show you sin, you bastard. You come with me to the town court right away.

I am not going.

You better, said the peasant, and he grabbed one wood plank and held it in his hands.

What, you old khui, you are threatening me?

Yes, I'm threatening you, you durak!

Grisha swung his axe and it whistled in the air; he was not really intending to split the peasant's head, but to ward him off like a horsefly. And if he hit the peasant, he could finish the job that someone had started earlier—cutting through his head.

The peasant also swung and he connected—hit Grisha right between the eyes and over the nose. Grisha went down. Light flickered red in his eyes, warmth enveloped him. He felt very comfortable so bathed in light and blood.

He passed out, though a smile stayed on his face.

He came to as the peasant was feeling his neck, chest, and hands for signs of life. As Grisha opened his eyes, he felt a hard-on coming. It was cold, and he realized that in his fall his pants had slipped down.

You swine, I thought you were dead, said the peasant, both relieved and disgusted. You are a dog, just a dirty dog.

Grisha watched him in a beatitudinous state, in pain and pleasure.

He stood up. Above the brown hair of the peasant, who seemed to be a mirage arising out of the mud, he beheld a sight from before: the boughs spread like huge arms; welcoming arms, looming in the light. They were thick black arms, with refracting light thinning them. The arms of the tree appeared to him to be the arms of Jesus in disguise, resurrected Jesus, who was nailed onto a tree, having come from the trees, as a carpenter's son.

This was a call from God to go out and worship the wood, the nature that grows out of the ground, the resurrected soil.

From a distance, a bell tolled and the beautiful sound of metal buzzed over the valley. The vibrations of the air penetrated Grisha's ears and shook his loosened nose bones, so that his nose hurt even more. He snorted out blood, and his horse snorted on the road, in sympathy.

Grisha decided he would be a carpenter, like Jesus, and Jesus would live in him as long as he cut wood.

Why are you staring at me like that? You have brain damage? You damned thief!

You think that my collecting wood is stealing, but it is no stealing.

It's theft and destruction of property.

The whole land and all the wood belong to God. It's brazen of people to imagine that it is theirs. The people have stolen from God, and I aim to return the wood to God.

What people? You mean me? The peasant punched him on his left cheekbone.

Grisha saw lightning.

Why are you grinning, fucker! You falling asleep?

Oh, no, on the contrary. This has been an awakening for me.

You call that awakening? The peasant pointed downward. Pack it away, you dog. And wash it. That's my advice.

Spiritual awakening. I have seen the light.

All right. You'll get even more awakening at the magistrate's office. Let's go. Poshli!

Grisha knelt to the ground, crossed himself with two fingers, and said, Thank you, Lord.

Don't you have three fingers? asked the peasant. Don't pretend to be a believer, old or new.

Grisha stood up and said, I will follow you. I am a sinner and I am ready for justice.

Now you are willing?

Yes. And if you want, hit me again with that wood. You can punish me.

I could kill you and that wouldn't restore my fence.

Oh, you couldn't kill me. Please hit me again.

Why?

I deserve it.

I could, but it wouldn't do much good. At court, you will pay me back the damages, and you have to build me another fence. And maybe you can work for me as a swineherd.

Gladly. That's a wonderful job for a prodigal son.

You motherfucker, don't give yourself no fancy names now. You have nothing to do with religion.

You'd be surprised. I've just got a call from the Lord.

The peasant spat. At least you seem strong enough to do some work.

On the way to the courthouse, Grisha kept smiling and seeing visions of naked dancing angels. Most of them were female, and they had wonderfully loose breasts. Oh, thank you, Lord, he said. I thought angels were men.

What the fuck are you talking about? asked the peasant.

I am not talking to you, but to the Lord.

He looked at the trees above them, the boughs embracing the road ahead. He was a sinner, expiating for his sins in his own blood and the blood of Christ. He would be born again through this bloodbath and light; his old self would die, and the new one would be born. This was more complete than St. Paul's conversion on the way to Damascus, which didn't include baptism in blood.

He inhaled with delight the blood through his nose. It made strange slurping sounds. The peasant watched him with disgust.

My friend, you are a Godsend to me, said Grisha. You have no idea how beautiful this all is. May I kiss you?

The peasant pushed him and hit him on the nape with his fist.

Oh, thank you. I deserve this and more. I have been truly evil. Do you drink vodka?

Are you offering?

No. God doesn't want us to drink anymore. It is an evil drink.

How would you know? You look drunk to me.

I was, but Lord has sobered me up through your gracious fist. You know, I am not going to pollute the temple of the Holy Ghost, my body, by eating meat and drinking vodka.

The peasant kicked him in the ass and said, You call this temple?

I will eat only vegetables of the fields.

That's fine, but don't steal mine.

And moreover, fish.

He didn't remember that Jesus had eaten anything but figs, fish, and unleavened bread. Maybe he drank some red wine, but where would Grisha get red wine? The Siberian climate didn't welcome red grapes.

In order to dedicate himself to the matters of the spirit, he would need a wife, a sturdy one. He had admired the miller on the outskirts of the village who didn't need anything, other than the nails, from the Czardom. The rest he generated in his mill, and what he couldn't do, his powerful wife did. He boasted she was better and stronger than the mule—somewhat more intelligent and much more powerful. She could lift a mule, and she could till the ground and grow vegetables. And not only that: she bore him five children, and after each birth, she'd get up in ten minutes and go back to the field to till some more.

Now Grisha asked the peasant, Do you have any daughters? Perhaps I could marry one when I work as a laborer for you.

Yes, I have ten of them. You may not look at them. You touch one of them, I will nail your ass to a spruce—I'll fucking crucify you.

Grisha inhaled deeply, slurping. A drop of thick blood got caught in his windpipe and he coughed, and as he coughed his nose seemed to be splitting in sheer luminous pain.

www.ingramcontent.com/pod-product-compliance
Lightning Source LLC
Chambersburg PA
CBHW021721190726
48289CB00008B/2633
9781738654833